Appreciation Marketing™

How to Achieve Greatness Through Gratitude

Tommy Wyatt & Curtis Lewsey

"My family built its entire business on the principles of appreciation and gratitude. Tommy and Curtis don't just hug their customers, they hug everybody! Their message isn't only refreshing; it's essential to success in today's marketplace."

—*Jack Mitchell, CEO*
Mitchell's/Richard's/Marsh's;
Author of Hug Your Customers

Book design by Marian Hartsough Associates
Cover design by BFC Group Publishing

ISBN: 978-0-9824663-0-8
Printed in the United States of America

10 9 8 7 6 5 4 3 2

BFC GROUP PUBLISHING
P.O. BOX 682
Westport, CT 06881
(800) 247-6553
www.appreciationmarketing.com

Contents

11   Answer to Your Prayers   85

12   It's Always Sunny Above the Clouds   91

13   In my Next Life, I'm Coming Back as *Me!*   99

14   The Popcorn Principle   105

15   Build it and They Will Come
      (Formulate your AMS)   111

      Epilogue   121

      About the Authors   124

      Acknowledgments   127

Foreword

When Curtis and I decided to sit down and write this book, it wasn't out of desire and it certainly wasn't for the money. We didn't dream up the idea, create an outline, and hire a ghost writer. And it wasn't a prompting. Funny as it sounds, the decision to actually go ahead and put these words on paper felt more like a responsibility. A calling, if you will.

The two of us had begun a direct-selling adventure back in April of 2007, marketing for a multi-million dollar company that specializes in appreciation and relationship building. We were promoted quickly and within seven months we became corporate trainers. In doing so, we had the awesome pleasure of traveling North America teaching the Law of Attraction principles that our company was built on and—as we found—all other companies *should* be built on as well.

As we continued to share this message in our everyday travels, we found that these ideas came off as fresh and cutting edge. We discovered that although the principles of appreciation had really been around forever, most people in business had completely gotten away from them.

Then we began to get testimonials from people who, in just days after applying our principles, experienced life-changing results and couldn't stop thanking us.

One woman was struggling with her real estate business and sat down with us for lunch. We talked about the principles of Appreciation Marketing and even shared with her a mechanism with which to incorporate them. Three days after our lunch, she earned a $2.4 million listing seemingly out of the clear blue sky.

Another woman, in southern California, was so enamored with these principles that she asked our assistance in helping roll them out with her entire company (a large insurance firm). Sure enough, within months, numbers shot up and the appreciation was coming back to them exponentially.

A young girl, fresh out of college, had just interviewed for a huge job with a major television network. After about fifteen minutes of talking about our principles we decided it would be a great idea to send a "thank you" card to her interviewer. She got the job.

A friend who sells private jets for a living, and deals with very high-net-worth clients, began using our appreciation principles and started getting his foot in the door with business titans that he previously couldn't get anywhere near. Now *they* (not their secretaries) were personally calling *him* to set up appointments.

We've lectured on the principles of Appreciation Marketing in front of BNI groups, Chambers of Commerce, and numerous other networking groups around New York and New England and invariably the results have been the same. Eyes (and sometimes mouths) wide open, notes being taken at a fever pitch, and more than anything else . . . results.

It was for that reason that the two of us decided to put our brains together and just take everything we've been preaching and get it down in book format. In the pages that follow you will expose yourself to all of our principles of Appreciation Marketing. Though the words and the stories will be coming from my mouth (and fingers) in the first person, everything you read and hear is a collaboration of our combined experience.

The message that follows needs to be shared, not only for the success of business, but for the betterment of mankind. We're not so naïve that we think we can actually change the world, as a whole. But we all don't live in the same world. Curtis and I sincerely believe that each one of us, as individuals, live in a world all our own. And not only do we all hold the desire to better that world, but we also possess the ability to.

Our hope is that we can help point you in that direction.

We appreciate you!

— Tommy & Curtis

CHAPTER ONE

Appreciation Marketing: What is it?

"Appreciation wins out over self promotion every single time."

—*Kody Bateman*

In the spirit of the resurgence of Indiana Jones, the quest continues on for that Holy Grail which is known to business owners as "customer loyalty."

To find it, you won't need a whip and a gun and a 60-something-year-old action hero. No, instead you can secure a lifetime of customer loyalty by exercising a little common sense. What makes *you* a loyal customer is what will make your customers loyal customers. Hmm, why didn't I think of that?

What makes me loyal to my utility companies? The answer is: nothing. I speak for most people when I say that I truly do not care who my phone company, my cable company, and my electric company are. They're just who I've been using and I stay with them because the daunting idea of switching gives me the fever sweats.

The same thing holds true for my bank, my internet provider, and my cell phone. I'm locked in.

I'm not partial to which gas station I stop at. It's which ever one's the most convenient at the time. I don't care who mows my lawn, who plows my driveway, who does my dry cleaning, or who washes my car.

When I fly, I absolutely do not care which airline I travel with. There are some I won't fly with, like one in particular who is completely insensitive to my peanut allergy, but who I *do* fly with usually comes down to price point.

Enough already!

Let's examine the other side of the coin.

I *am* faithful to my Realtor. I only use one plumber. I have an insurance agent, a mortgage guy, a painter, an accountant, a lawyer, a financial planner, a mechanic, a caterer, and a jeweler. I'm theirs for life. I'm "loyal."

What is it that sets these professionals apart from the others? They know my name. They care about me as a human being. They are grateful for my business. And, because of all that, I like them!

These professionals were strangers when I first hired them. I now consider them friends. They send me birthday and holiday cards. They're always polite on the phone and happy to see me in person.

Can the answer really be that simple? Yes. A recent study showed that 68% of customers who "leave," do so because of perceived indifference.

I remember opening my first bank account back in 1980. Every single time I walked into that bank I was greeted first by the bank manager and second by a smiling teller, both of whom knew my name. They also knew the names of my family members, where I worked, and what I liked to do for fun. Just like the old *Cheers* jingle, *Sometimes you want to go where everybody knows your name. And they're always glad you came.*

I used to love going into that bank.

The bank has since been bought out by a bigger conglomerate no fewer than five times, and I'm 100% certain that not a single employee there could pick me out of a police lineup. I'm still a customer today. Not because I'm loyal. In fact, as I write this I'm committing myself to taking a day off (or however long it takes) and transferring my fortunes—*wink*—to a new bank.

But will they be any better?

Companies today are squandering millions of dollars searching for that elusive Grail, when it's as simple, and inexpensive, as a little human touch.

To paraphrase a credit card company that falls into the "guilty of total indifference" column:

> *A smile and a sincere 60-second phone call once every six months: Two cents.*
>
> *A heartfelt birthday card and a personal, hand written holiday card once a year: Three dollars.*
>
> *An endless referral source disguised as your customer for life: Priceless.*

Hence, this book you hold in your hands right now. We know what you're thinking. "Appreciation Marketing, hmm, sounds very appealing. How come I've never heard this term before?"

You've heard of direct marketing, internet marketing, niche marketing, network marketing, relationship marketing, viral marketing, mass marketing, information marketing, e-mail marketing, social marketing, lifestyle marketing, buzz marketing, and good old marketing marketing, which you can major in at college. Now we even have integration marketing and even mind-control marketing. But never Appreciation Marketing.

Wonder why?

Well, up until now it didn't exist—as a term, anyway. But today's fast-paced business world has created an evolution of sorts, a little *Back to the Future* action if you will. Principles that were so commonplace twenty, thirty, forty years ago have been replaced by computers, email, FAX machines, PDAs, and voice messaging.

That once handwritten Nice to Meet You greeting card has been replaced by a robotic email or text message. That once heartfelt Happy Birthday phone call is now left on the answering machine. Everything is done faster, faster, and faster than ever before because we perceive it has to be. It's the new millennium.

Alas, all this wonderful technology that was supposed to open the door to new horizons and make your business life easier has instead double-crossed you.

Ever heard of Google?

Today we're living in a Google world. Think about it; whatever product or service you sell or represent can be found online better and cheaper than you offer it, in twenty seconds and two mouse clicks. So what is it, I ask, that keeps your customers loyal to you and your company? Is there really a way, a practice, that would help you put the "high touch" back into this "high tech" world?

Yep. It's called Appreciation Marketing.

Building better and stronger relationships with your inner circle and your client base is more important today than it ever was before. Not only is it fundamentally wise, but where your present and future success is concerned, it's essential.

It sounds so obvious. It goes back to Mark Twain's old quote, *"I don't know why they call it common sense. It really isn't all that common."* This, consequently, is a book filled with common sense.

As you read these pages it will all become crystal clear to you. Please realize that the real superstars of your industry already practice these principles. The most successful business people in your town already know this stuff. Why didn't they tell you about it? Maybe they have been. Maybe you just haven't been paying attention.

The good news is, all that is about to change.

CHAPTER TWO

You *Should* Have Said 'Thank You'!

"Feeling gratitude and not expressing it is like wrapping a present and not giving it."

—*William Arthur Ward*

Remember the last time you went out of your way to go the extra mile for somebody? Remember doing something so exceptional, so over the top, that you just couldn't wait to get that person's reaction?

And you waited.

And you waited.

And you waited.

Finally, you bumped into that person. Still, nothing.

Then *you* brought it up.

"Oh yeah, thanks, that was great."

How about that last traffic incident?

You figured you be the nice guy and let that other car pull out ahead of you. As it did so, you watched the driver's every gesture. You didn't even know the person, but you yearned for (and expected) that little thank you wave.

"What? No wave? Jerk!!!"

Then there was that time you splurged. You spent a little more than you intended on that wedding gift, or that special birthday gift. You just knew they were going to love it. You just couldn't wait for their reaction.

And you waited.

And you waited.

And you waited.

How did that make you feel?

What did that make you think of that person?

Were you excited to go out of your way again?

Chances are, that's the last good deed that person ever receives from you.

The truth is, *not* saying thank you does more damage than actually *saying* thank you does good.

I once had a next-door neighbor who was the sales manager at a car dealership. When I wanted a new SUV, I went to his dealership and bought it from him. I then referred five different people to him, all of whom purchased cars. One of them, my brother-in-law Marc, has now purchased three different cars there. Can you believe that my neighbor has never once even said thank you for the business? Not only has he not thanked me, or shown any type of appreciation at all, he's never even acknowledged the fact that he's sold NINE cars directly through me.

The ironic thing is, the four-year lease on my Yukon Denali is about to expire and I'm considering a Nissan 350-Z Convertible. If I'm still thinking Nissan in five months, you can be sure of one place where I will *not* be buying it.

So what about you?

Be honest.

How often do *you* say thank you? No, really. Sometimes? Once in a while? When it's convenient? Hmmmm. *Always?*

The fact is, even the best of us, in this age of multi-tasking and the 80-hour work week, have found a way to cheapen (or expedite) the gesture of saying thank you. We can thank the invention of the internet and the world wide web, because email is partially to blame. And while an emailed thank you is better than no appreciation at all, it has come to be recognized as a path of least resistance. It will suffice, but it doesn't do much to set you apart.

What do *you* do to set yourself apart? Isn't that what successful business is all about? Have you implemented an "Appreciation Marketing Strategy" (AMS) into your business? Most people have great intentions but admit that they are horrible with the follow-through. Again, our fast-paced lifestyles have rendered card sending and note writing to be costly, inconvenient, and time consuming.

In the business arena though, especially today, those age-old words—*thank you*—have given companies and individuals a serious edge in the marketplace. Simple heartfelt thank you messages have created a competitive advantage. When was the last time you got a personal greeting card in the mailbox? When was the last time you had a handwritten card placed on your desk, on your windshield, on your door, or even on your pillow? A little better than an email, huh?

Champions of 'Thank You'

Mary Kay Ash, founder of Mary Kay Cosmetics, built a $1.2 billion cosmetics empire because she understood the importance of gratitude. Her personal philosophy, which she taught to her sales reps, was to send out three handwritten thank you notes every night before bed.

This practice not only expressed her gratitude to the people she met with and did business with, but also allowed her to maintain a positive attitude all day long as she sought out people to whom she'd send these thank you notes.

Today, Mary Kay Cosmetics has 1.5 million sales people in 32 countries. She knew how to harness the power of thank you.

Another sales superstar who built a multi-million dollar empire on the power of thank you notes is Tom Hopkins.

At the age of nineteen, Hopkins was a construction worker. Not wanting to spend the rest of his life doing physical labor, he quit that job and took one he thought would be easier, selling real estate.

Six months into his real estate career, his income was averaging less than $50 a month. He wasn't earning a living, but had fallen in love with the real estate business.

After discovering that all the top producers had extensive sales training, Tom set out to learn everything he could about how to sell professionally.

He developed a habit of sending out ten hand-written thank you cards every single day and within the next five years built his annual sales volume to over $14 million a year. He credits the thank-you habit for creating a business that was built on 99% warm referrals.

To date, Hopkins has sold over 1.4 million copies of his books worldwide and has conducted sales seminars for over four million people on five continents.

He's clearly another evolved character whose understanding of the power of Appreciation Marketing made him an overwhelming success in life.

Clearly sending notes and cards isn't the only way to say thank you. But it just might be the best way.

A phone call is nice, an email does the trick, but it's the actual note or card that sets you apart big time. Think about it. You hang up the phone. You delete the email. But what do you do with the card? Yeah, many times it gets thrown away, but how many old greeting cards do you have around that you've saved—for whatever reason? There's something about a heartfelt note or greeting card that makes a person feel special. Sort of like a photo album.

"I have three drawers in my desk, on the right hand side, that are filled with cards and letters people have written to me over the years," says Dave Polstra, founding partner of Brightworth, a thriving independent financial firm in Atlanta, Georgia.

"It's been my experience that people really appreciate it when you take the time to send them a card or a personal note," he says. "We all go to our mailbox every day and what are we looking for? We're not looking for the junk mail or the bills. We're looking for the personal mail. That all seems to have gotten lost today. When you get a personal letter from someone it has a significant meaning to it."

It's his wisdom and professional ethic that have propelled Polstra to be recognized by *Worth* Magazine as one of the top 250 financial advisors in America. But it's his penchant for appreciation that has allowed him to set himself apart with his clientele. Though he has been a card sender for many years, Polstra has taken his acts of appreciation to another level. He actually has custom cards made with personal photographs on the front.

"Everybody thinks I'm this conservative, stoic, financial planner," he quips. "Then they get these custom birthday cards from me, with personal pictures on them, and they remember it. These clients save the cards I send them and they bring it up all the time."

And not only does Polstra practice Appreciation Marketing principles himself, but he also recommends it to the twenty-six agents throughout his two offices. "We think of our clients as glasses half-filled with water," he explains. "Every day you are either putting more water in, or taking some out. It takes years to build a relationship with a client, but can take only seconds to lose it."

Perhaps great American writer Maya Angelou said it best when she offered that unforgettable quote: *"I've learned that people will forget what you said, people will forget what you did, but people will never forget how you made them feel."*

Better Late Than Never

So you forgot to say thank you.

Yeah, it happens to the best of us.

You got that gift and you meant to send a special thank you card, so you didn't verbally say thank you. Then you got sidetracked and you forgot to send it, and now three months have gone by.

Suddenly, you're in the grocery store and you see that person you forgot to thank wheeling their carriage towards you. You're so embarrassed, you pretend not to see them and completely blow off the condiments aisle.

So back at home, in addition to being without ketchup for another week, you're faced with a protocol issue. When is it too late to say thank you? The answer is: Never.

The proper thing to do would be to send a thank you note and apologize for it being late. Tell that person about how you've been thinking about them and their wonderful gesture and have been meaning to get out that thank you, but life got in the way. You'll come off like a star. Problem solved.

On time is best. But late is okay too. In fact, when it comes to gratitude, *late* is a hundred times better than *never*.

We recently ran a Law of Attraction seminar in North Carolina. It was well attended and upon returning home, we received many thank you, and nice-to-meet you cards from people who were in attendance. In this case, no card was required, but every card went a long way towards people setting themselves apart as quality individuals. Certainly, every card was appreciated.

Three months later, a card arrived in the mail. It was from a couple who attended that seminar. It read:

> *"Although this card is way overdue, we wanted to thank you so much for the wonderful presentation you gave. We have been to many seminars, but never had seen you. I must say that you guys were phenomenal. You way exceeded our expectations. Our key guy had never been to a seminar and he really loved it and so did we. You were inspirational, motivational, and very entertaining! You are a true representation of what the Law of Attraction is all about!"*

What would you feel like if you got a card like that? Even if it was late? Agreed! It's never too late to receive a message like that one!

"Better late than never."

I wonder who the person was who actually came up with that saying? Let's reflect for a minute on the "never" part of that term.

I have a friend who owns an online travel business. For no other reason, except that we are friends, I went to his website just as I was about to book a trip out west. First, I went directly to the popular travel sites and checked out airfare. Next, I went to his site and looked up the same flights and hotels. What I discovered was that the prices were pretty similar and his, in fact, was a little bit less expensive.

He didn't know it at the time, but I booked my trip through his website, thus earning him whatever commission his company pays out. I was so excited to hear back from him because I knew how happy he was going to be. I planned to tell him how pleased I was with the process and the good deal I got. I was even prepared to book through his site exclusively for the foreseeable future, and even refer my friends and associates.

Problem was, I NEVER heard from him. Not only did he never thank me for my business, he never even acknowledged that I had actually done it. I began to wonder if he ever even *knew*.

Finally, a few months later, I broke down and shot him an email. "Did you get credit for the trip I booked through your website?"

He replied, "Yes, take a look at some of the new deals that are on there right now."

On my next trip, I used his company again—but booked it through a different agent's website. And now that I think about it, that other agent didn't say thank you either.

This is a perfect example about how *not* saying thank you is even worse than actually saying thank you is good. If somebody perceives you as ungrateful, they look at you in a negative light and are less likely to do business with you ever again.

What to say "thank you" for . . .

This shouldn't be a tricky subject at all. The answer is: Everything!

As children we're constantly being scolded to say "please" and "thank you." And it's for our own good!

These are some of the very first words that we're taught. Kids naturally (because they learn it from the adults around them) say "Gimme this, gimme that." They say "It's MINE!" They say "I WANT this, I WANT that!" In fact, they sound a lot like the business people of today. Well, the ones who don't 'get it' anyway. And our parents just kept on coaching. "Say please. Pleeeeease. Say Please. You don't get it until you say please!"

"Now say thank you." "Thank you." "Say thank you, sweetie!" "If you don't say thank you, you won't get any more."

Remember how impressed you were the last time you witnessed a young child using manners?

BULLSEYE! Mom and dad *did* know something!

As we become parents, it starts all over again. "Say Please, sweetie!" "Now say Thank you!"

Eventually, somebody gets the point! And invariably, the please part gets overused . . . and even annoying. But nobody gets tired of Thank You.

Not ever.

The Appreciation Marketing genius is creative when it comes to the subject of thank you. Not only is he automatic in expressing the *expected* thank yous, but he's constantly finding ways to convey the *unexpected* thank yous that have far more impact.

Think about it. You expect a thank you when you give somebody a gift or go out of your way in some capacity. But how often do you receive a thank you from somebody for something small or even something profound?

A "something small" could be: Thank you for meeting me for coffee. Something "profound" might be: Thank you for being a positive influence on my life or my business career.

In either case, the expected thank yous are important—but they are expected. However it's unexpected gratitude that sets you apart as an extraordinary human being. It's the type of appreciation that creates warm feelings toward you and is then passed along to others.

The "Next Level" of Thank You

I think we've driven home our point on the importance of saying thank you. But we should also point out that there are varying degrees of thank you.

First you have the words, "thank you."

Second you have a gesture, like a phone call, a greeting card, or a personal note; both expected and unexpected.

And, finally, we have the *next level* of thank you; the gift. There is no classier expression of gratitude than to include a gift with a heartfelt thank you.

It doesn't have to be a Ferrari. In fact it can be as simple as a cup of coffee, a cigar, a flower, a gift card, or a piece of candy.

I see pharmaceutical sales reps all the time, wheeling carts full of sandwiches for medical offices. Financial planners often cater lunches for their clients. Realtors pass out boxes of candy and calendars during the holidays. When given properly, gifts really pack a punch.

When Curtis Lewsey—this book's co-author—graduated from Sacred Heart University in 2005, he took a sales job selling business-to-business services for a multi-billion dollar corporation as a means to gain "real world" sales experience.

"I was taught to be a hunter," he explains. "Every day was all about getting new business and you were only as good as your last sale. When new business was written, it was turned over to the service department and I was paid a one-time commission for that sale. I was trained to look at people and accounts as dollar signs and numbers.

"After a year of starting over again every single day, every week, every month, every quarter, I started to get burned out. Although I was very good at what I did, there was no enjoyment in it whatsoever. Something big was missing. And that something was relationships."

Curtis made a decision to start focusing on relationship building, using an actual appreciation strategy, and the results came quickly. In his second year, he worked half the hours and was still able to maintain the same income level because of his newfound philosophy.

"One day I received a lead from a service driver," Curtis remembers. "The lead never worked out, but I was so appreciative that this guy would give *me* a lead. On the way back to the office that day I swung by a Subway, picked up a foot-long meatball sub, and left it in his locker with a sticky note that said only two words: Thank You. "

That night, the driver called Curtis and expressed *his* thanks for the thoughtful gesture. He was amazed that Curtis had remembered his mentioning that he liked the meatball subs at Subway.

The following week the driver passed along two more referrals. This time, though, they did pan out. One, in fact, came with a four-figure commission that pushed Curtis into a different bonus tier with his company. This push resulted in an additional $3,000 bonus and made Curtis Lewsey a six-figure income earner in only his second year out of college.

"The other salesmen considered me lucky," Curtis says, "But that wasn't the end of it. The stories just kept on piling up. The service department kept on coming to me first, and passing *me* referrals. I had created a competitive edge over everyone in my office because I understood the importance of gratitude and appreciation. I didn't give the gift because I was trying to get something in return. But as it turned out, my return on a six dollar sandwich was several thousand percent!"

Dr Steven Covey's *The 7 Habits of Highly Effective People* was named the #1 Most Influential Business Book of the Twentieth Century. In his newest book, *Everyday Greatness*, Covey wrote:

> *In terms of the energy and know-how required, gratitude is one of the easiest of all principles to apply. Though it also generally returns rich dividends, it is vastly underutilized. Why? Perhaps because of a lack of humility—It can be hard to acknowledge the need to be helped. Or a lack of courage—a person might be too shy to tell another how much he or she means. Yet, people with Everyday Greatness are quick to exhibit everyday gratitude. They do not take life or the kindness of others for granted. They are eager to say thanks and among the first to express praise.*

The Appreciator

. . . Expresses Gratitude

Take out a pen and write down the name of one person you forgot to thank recently. Its okay, even the pros commit errors. The good news is that your sharpened sense of awareness will soon make it impossible for you to forget again.

Now think of somebody who could have, or should have, thanked YOU for something recently but—for whatever reason—did not. How does that make you feel? Our advice is to give them the benefit of the doubt. They were too busy, they forgot, they might even still be meaning to thank you. The important thing here is to make sure that nobody is left wondering why YOU haven't been grateful.

Finally, write down the name of somebody who you could thank for something TODAY. You can do it. You'll see an instant change in your life if you begin this practice and make it into a lifelong habit.

CHAPTER THREE

If Only I *Liked* You . . .

"Likeability may well be the deciding factor in every competition you'll ever enter."

—*Tim Sanders*

We, as consumers, are a heck of a lot smarter than we're given credit for.

We know when we're being lied to.

We know when we're being sold to.

We can recognize insincerity like the big bad wolf dressed up in grandma's red flannel nightgown.

So if *we're* so smart—don't you think the same can be said for *our* customers too?

I've always gotten a kick out of watching the political debates on television. The candidates stand up there and promise this and promise that.

"If I'm elected, blah blah blah blah blah."

This, of course, is followed by the opponent saying, "Then why did you do this and that, and vote this way for this and that, and never stand up for this and that in the past?"

Hmm, great question.

The truth is, most politicians, like most business people, have the best of intentions. They're very skilled and polished at telling you what you want to hear, but only when it suits *them*. But the most successful politicians and salespeople should be able proudly say, "I'm going to do this and do that, just like I've been doing all my life; just like I've been doing all along." Wouldn't that be a breath of fresh air?

That stuff, by the way, is called integrity. Honesty. Sincerity. We don't see it a lot anymore, but the good news is it can be earned back.

My father always used to accuse me, *"You only call me when you want something."* Guilty as charged. But it's not my fault. And it's probably not your fault. Well, not totally.

We get so mixed up in our busy lives. We're so ambitious. We're so busy looking for *new* business and trying to build *new* relationships that we forget to take care of our *existing* business and foster our *existing* relationships.

But how do you do it?

Remember the dating scene?

What kinds of things did you do to win over that girl or guy you had your eye on?

You were probably on top of your game as far as personal hygiene was concerned. You probably dressed nicely and smiled a lot. You went out of your way to say and do nice things for that person. You wrote notes, sent cards, left up-beat messages, and even said you were sorry when it clearly wasn't your fault!

You found a way to get out of work to meet for lunch. You did everything in your power to be thoughtful and charming and, even if you played a little "hard-to-get," you still found a way to amplify your best qualities tenfold, and somehow put your worst qualities into a lockbox. I didn't pass wind for five years when I first met my wife!

Clearly this is an extreme example, but one that most everybody can relate to. Is it that difficult to be likeable?

In his book, *The Likeability Factor*, Tim Sanders, the Chief Solutions officer at Yahoo!, hits the nail right on the head. "Our nation is so focused on efficiency and productivity that we forget that likeability is truly our lifeline," he wrote. "People who are likeable, or who have what I call a high *L-factor*, tend to land jobs more easily, find friends more quickly, and have happier relationships. I now believe that having a high L-factor isn't just a way to improve your life, it's a way to save it."

There has actually been research conducted at major U.S. universities on the topic of likeability, and studies have shown that success in the workplace is directly correlated to popularity. People who get the big promotions, the nicer offices, and the bigger opportunities are the people who are more well-liked. Conversely, those who are less-liked are perceived as arrogant, conniving, and manipulative and are the ones more often passed over for promotions and are the first ones sent packing during layoffs.

A 2000 Yale University study showed that the majority of today's successful business leaders attained their edge through likeability. They make it a habit to treat their customers, employees, colleagues, and associates with respect and they get the same in return.

Jack Mitchell, CEO of Mitchell's, Richard's, and Marsh's, three of the most successful high-end clothing stores in the industry, totaling more than $100 Million annually, has written two books on gratitude. His first best seller was called *Hug Your Customers*. It told how his family built a multi-million dollar clothing empire through the principles of gratitude and appreciation. His follow-up book, *Hug Your People* was his answer to the question; how do you establish a "hug-your-customers" environment within the workplace?

Mitchell and his family have always practiced appreciation principles and have always treated their customers and associates as human beings. Because of this philosophy they have reaped the rewards, even in down markets.

In this "hugging" environment, it isn't a strange occurrence to see customers actually being hugged in these Connecticut and New York stores. "We mainly metaphorically hug them by showering them with attention in a way that every business ought to, but doesn't," writes Mr. Mitchell in *Hug Your Customers*. "We've been told by others that we're one of the most successful—if not the most successful—high-end clothing business of our size in the country, and maybe in the world. It's not because of our product, it's not because of our prices—other stores have great product at the same prices—it's because of how we personally treat customers."

"Our vision," he said, "is that anyone that becomes a customer of our stores enters an enduring relationship with us. He or she instantly becomes our friend."

Likeability isn't just important in business.

University studies have also concluded that marriages in which one or both spouses are friendly, laid back, and likeable people are much less likely to end in divorce. In fact, when one spouse possesses these likeability qualities, the divorce rate is 50% less than the national average. When both do, that number jumps to 75%.

Where else can likeability help you? Doctors have been found to give more of their time, and advice, to patients they like. Diners in restaurants get better service when they're friendlier. In fact, regardless of the area in question, the door opens wider—every single time—for the person who is perceived as friendlier and is consequently more likeable.

How many presidential elections can you recall?

Go ahead, try.

While thinking about these elections, take a minute to consider the candidate's L-Factor (as Tim Sanders would put it).

I can personally recall campaigns from nine presidential elections, but can also easily use history to help me date back to the very beginning in 1776. Consider those elections and how likeability played a role.

In the nine campaigns I can recall, including the most recent with Barack Obama, I can confidently say that likeability may be THE most important quality in getting elected. Funny, I can hardly even remember any of the campaign promises!

David Stern, commissioner of the National Basketball Association, took a page out of Maya Angelou's book when he said, "It isn't completely important what people think about you. It is, however, totally important how they feel about you."

He's right.

If you want to figure out a way to grow a never-ending, continuously-growing, flourishing business—in any industry—then you need to think like an educated consumer (aka a human being), instead of an eager business person.

You need to internalize what *every* consumer thinks. . .

"I'd be happy to do business with you . . . if only I liked you!"

The Appreciator

. . . is a Magnetic Person

Think of three people you like, right now. Take a few minutes and write their names down on a piece of paper. What is it about those people that you like? List the qualities. You'll probably come up with things like upbeat, fun, honest, successful, positive, attractive, confident, funny, thoughtful, and (wait for it . . .) they like YOU! Isn't it strange that we tend to like people who like us? After all, if they like you then they're obviously pretty smart, right?!

It's just logical that you like being around people who think that you're a wonderful person. We love to see people who put us in a good mood. We like people who compliment us and go out of their way to include us and recognize us. So, if *we* like it, doesn't it stand to reason that that's what *other* people like in a person as well? How hard, then, would it truly be to become a person that other people like? It's just a choice.

CHAPTER FOUR

Seven Deadly Creatures

"Man . . . is a tame or civilized animal; never the less, he requires proper instruction and a fortunate nature, and then of all animals he becomes the most divine and most civilized; but if he be insufficiently or ill- educated he is the most savage of earthly creatures."

—Plato

Have you ever gone on an African safari? Have you camped at Yellowstone Park or anywhere in the great Northwest? Have you trekked the Amazon basin? Okay, me neither. Have you ever watched the Discovery Channel? If so, you'll remember your tour guide giving you a short-list of creatures that you must avoid confrontation with at all costs. This list includes things like lions and tigers and bears, anything poisonous, and of course any mother protecting her young.

There are certain creatures to avoid in business as well. You know who they are. And chances are good that you know all of them. Let me stress, that these are—in many cases—really good people. They're human beings with positive qualities and they absolutely deserve your appreciation.

It's okay to know them, and it's even okay to do business with them. The important thing, though—where *your* Appreciation Marketing Strategy is concerned—is that you don't *become* one of them!

If you do, your career—and your personal life—will be in grave danger.

The Sucker

There's an old poker aphorism that says, "If you can't spot the sucker at the table within ten minutes—it's *you*!" Well, we're not talking about that kind of "sucker" here.

Picture it. Your cell phone rings in your pocket, you scramble to grab it, and before answering you look down at the 'Caller ID' number on the display. "Uggggh!" You let this one roll to voicemail. It's one of those Energy Suckers!

You know exactly who we're talking about! This person is such an energy sucker that just the sight of their phone number on the screen puts you in a negative state. Of course you don't answer it. And you might not even return this call. Certainly not right away.

Now the big question . . . drum roll please . . . how do people react when they look down at their phone and see *your* phone number? Are you a sucker?

Clearly it's a strong business tip to be an energy *giver*, not an energy *sucker*. Conversely, we all have people in our lives who we just love to see. People we just love to hear from. People we drop everything—no matter how important—to take their phone calls. You know who we mean.

It's important to acknowledge that energy suckers aren't necessarily bad people. They can be friends, valued business associates, valued customers, and yes, even family members. They might not even know that they're suckers! But, for whatever reason, the thought of interacting with them instantly throws your brain into shut down mode.

What do you suppose the reason is for this? How did these people become energy suckers? The answer is simple and it lies within the very question. Since all things and all people are made up of energy, and since what you give out is what you get back, the energy attached to you is simply a reflection of the type of person you are and work to become.

For example, there's a guy I know who sells insurance. I went to high school with him many years go. We weren't really friends, but he had an "okay energy" attached to him and when I'd see him around it was always a friendly "hello" from both ends.

Since we don't run in the same circles, I only run into this guy maybe once every few years. And, invariably, every time I run into him and we do the small talk thing, I receive a phone call from him asking to quote my insurance. Now I love talking about insurance about as much as I love going to the dentist's office for major gum surgery. So naturally, when I see this individual, or he calls me, it sucks my energy to the very core. He isn't interested in me. He isn't interested in how I'm doing. He isn't interested in how he might be able to help me out. He's mainly interested in making some money.

Now let's be clear; in his mind he may have convinced himself that he's interested in helping me by reducing my insurance payments. But he's absolutely not in "giving" mode. He's in "getting" mode. (See Chapter Five).

Incidentally, this guy's voice message is flashing on my machine right now. And I do *not* plan on returning the call.

To keep the examples alive, let's talk about your spouse. Is your spouse a giver or a sucker? When you see "Home" come up on your cell phone do you get the warm and fuzzies, or are you afraid to answer it? Is it bad news? Did you screw up? And, again, what type of energy comes through the other end of the phone when *you* call *your* spouse? Hello! It's (at least) half your fault!

There's an international real estate company called Keller Williams. I've never listed or purchased a house through them but have many friends around the country who work for them. No matter what office I call, they answer the phone by saying, *"It's a great day at Keller Williams! How may I direct your call?"* I love that! I try to just call there and hang up whenever I'm having a bad day!

Every person you know and every person you see has one of three types of energy attached; just like an atom (footnote, I skipped science in high school). It's either positive, negative, or it's neutral. Remember the old Will Rogers quote? "You never get a second chance to make a first impression." That's because the person you meet forms an opinion and attaches the energy instantly. It could be your appearance, your scent, your voice, your actions, or your intentions.

Does it really matter how many phone calls you make in a day? We don't think so. All that really matters is what type of energy you've attached to the phone call and to yourself.

Don't be a sucker!

The Appreciator

. . . Gives off Positive Energy

Take a few minutes here and make a list of three people who are energy suckers. It will take you ten seconds. Now, how about a list of energy givers? This is lots more fun.

Who are the people that you just love to hear from? Close your eyes for a minute. Think about sitting at your desk, or on your couch, and the phone rings. It's one of your energy givers. Relax and experience the emotions that come to mind right now. Isn't that awesome?

What would your business life be like if every time you made a phone call, the person on the other end experienced that same emotion? How about your personal life?

You have this power.

The Puker

You can walk into any Starbucks, sit down, close your eyes, and listen. The most prominent of the seven deadly creatures is definitely The Puker.

While The Puker is indigenous to any public meeting place worldwide, for some strange reason it can be found in Starbucks at any given time on any given day.

One of the most frightening things about The Puker is that, unless they are conscious of the warning signs, any person can morph into one in a matter of seconds. Nobody is immune.

The Puker is that person who, in all their excitement about something (perhaps a product or a service or an opportunity), figuratively throws up all over somebody—thus scaring them off indefinitely.

For example: Quite by surprise, I bumped into an old friend at (yes, really) Starbucks and he stopped at my table. I had my laptop out and was checking my email while waiting for someone on a business appointment. We spent a few minutes doing the small talk dance, and I made the mistake of asking what he was doing for work these days. His reply to the question came quickly, and without warning, and without pause!

"Oh I'm still working at GE, but I started a side-business dealing in all natural health and wellness products which are so important today because of the environment and the ozone and global warming and if that's not important enough people are all becoming so overweight and unhealthy that they're suffering diabetes and heart disease more than ever before and though people are always talking about getting back in shape and becoming healthier they go right out and hit the drive up window for that greasy fast food which does nothing but clog their arteries and make matters worse. . . . (longest sentence in history followed by his first actual breath). I just got started with XYZ company and we offer all these natural products that can only be found at the tops of trees in the deepest jungles of regions where no civilized human has ever gone before and these products reduce all the signs of aging and prevent all illness but the FDA won't let us claim that even though it's true and I (without taking that second breath yet, while reaching into his tote bag and pulling out a catalog the size of a telephone book—in one deft motion) can get you set up on any of these products and get you a special wholesale rate if you're ready to become a member today for just forty-nine dollars. (Second breath, finally)! What's more important to you between family, money, free time, church, and health? (Impressive, an actual question!) Well, if you think about it (not waiting for me to *think about it*) none of the first four matter without your health. Did you know that nobody on their death bed ever said 'I wish I had spent more time at work'? The best news is that you can get started in just under a minute by going online and I notice that you're actually online right now. Here, go to this website and let me show you how you can get started and take advantage of our online ordering system. Because I didn't tell you that in addition to adding forty or fifty years to your life (yes, he really said that) you also have the ability to make money with this company in fact I know a lot of people who make over a million dollars a year and all they do is just what I'm doing right now only they've done it for longer."

I was waiting for a short pause so I could blast him with a fire hose. I didn't have the heart to tell him that I would rather sleep on the floor in a public restroom than do what he's "doing right now . . ."

So I pulled the Emergency Escape Hatch. I asked him for his business card!

Believe it or not, I actually did send this guy a greeting card wishing him all the luck in the world in his new endeavor. I was hoping to find the words to tell him, in a tactful way, that success for him would be impossible unless he found a way to stop vomiting all over people!

Question: If that guy called me up and asked if I'd like to meet him for lunch (probably somewhere healthy) do you think I'd agree?

Answer: "NO FLIPPING WAY!!!!"

While he is highly visible in any "recruiting" or "sales" situation, The Puker is most frequently seen in Network Marketing or Direct Selling circles. And it's The Puker who, more often than not, gives those companies a bad name.

The Appreciator

. . . Controls His Enthusiasm

The sad thing is, I've been The Puker before. And I'm fairly certain that you've been The Puker as well. I mean, really. You're in a conversation with somebody who would be a great client, or associate, and during that conversation they give you the perfect lead in! I mean, it's gift wrapped! They're begging you to make your sales pitch! Begging! Here's what you do from now on. Bring up the fact that you have something that they may be interested in. "Now's not the best time, but do you have a business card? Let's try to get together for a few minutes this week or next." When you get back to your office, you can send them an email or a greeting card saying it was nice to see them.

It's simple. Dangle it out there and pull it back. If they don't bite, they're probably not really interested. Like my grandfather used to say, "just kiss the girls that are leaning toward you!"

Remember, swallow hard. Hold it back. Don't do it! Whatever you do, don't become The Puker!

The Topper

Everybody knows this beast.

The Topper is that person who, no matter what the situation, has to one-up you. Whenever you accomplish a goal or elate over a special achievement, there's The Topper to tell you how he or she did it just a little bit better.

The Topper isn't necessarily a braggart, and isn't necessarily doing it to demean your achievement. The Topper is an insecure person who has to let everybody know of his significance.

In most cases The Topper was a big sports star in high school, or was the homecoming king or queen (normally in another state). He used to bench press 350 pounds or scored 100 points in one basketball game even before they had a three-point line. The Topper cured cancer and then turned down the CEO promotion at her company because she didn't want to relocate. Your new car is nice, but The Topper used to have the limited edition XYZ Supercar with the titanium engine, fully loaded. Now, of course, he rides a donkey to work.

The Topper is harmless, really. He's kind of like pigeons outside McDonald's. He's not a threat other than the fact he's just so darned annoying. And therein lays the threat. If *you* are The Topper, stop it!

You will struggle in your efforts to attract people towards your business, your product, your service, or yourself.

A friend recently invited me over to see "his new toys". He was excited about his new home theater system. He told me about his new 52-inch plasma television set, his new Blu-ray disc player, and his new surround sound. The gleam in his eye was like a kid on Christmas.

"I'd *love* to come over and see it," I told him, all the while swallowing hard not to tell him that I just purchased a 65-inch plasma TV with the Blu-ray and the surround sound system. "It sounds awesome!"

Later in the conversation he asked me about my TV. "Oh I just have one of those old clunkers," I told him.

The Appreciator

. . . Lifts Other People Up

Lift other people up. When somebody tells you a story during a conversation (or especially if you're overhearing a conversation with somebody else) just let them bask in their moment, their own glow. Even if you can one-up them, what's the point? It won't make them, or anyone else in the room, think more positively of you. They probably won't believe you anyway. It's okay to let other people shine.

In fact, it's an art.

The Whiner

The Whiner is another creature that you never want to become, but we all know plenty of them. I often wonder if The Whiners even know that they are The Whiners?

I'm sure you don't need a detailed description here, other than to say that The Whiner is The Sucker on training wheels.

The Whiner is usually depressed. He usually has a story to tell about the flat tire on the freeway, the speeding ticket, the person who cut him off in traffic, the potholes in the road, the weather, the bad cell phone reception at his house, the neighbors, the people who are trying to take advantage of him, the government, the service at the restaurant, the food at the restaurant, the actual restaurant . . . I think you get the picture.

Not a lot of fun to be around, The Whiner. When you're in the market for whatever product or service he offers, you won't be calling The Whiner unless you just can't find anyone else.

Again, The Whiner is probably a nice person; a person who needs and deserves to love and be loved. In fact, you probably have (at least) one right in your very own family.

There's some great news for The Whiner, too. His condition is just a symptom of negative thinking. And it just so happens that "thinking" is the one and only thing we have control over in this world. So if diagnosed early enough, The Whiner can make the choice to stop complaining about all the taxes he's paying and just be happy that he won the lottery!

Remember, the difference between a Whiner and a Winner is just one letter.

The Appreciator

. . . Doesn't Complain

If this description fits you, congratulations for recognizing it! The good news is that you can make a few adjustments to go from a whiner to a winner. First, try to find a silver lining when something is bothering you. If you just can't, then keep it to yourself. It takes practice to become a good-finder. (More on this in Chapter 12)

It's important for you to know that when you complain about something, 80% of people don't care anyway. The other 20% are happy for you! The truth is that no matter what happens to you, somebody else out there has it a lot worse.

Narcissus

Narcissus is the boy in the Greek myth who, while leaning forward to drink from a pool in the forest, saw his own reflection and fell madly in love with himself.

To his credit, I guess, he didn't know it was him!

Where Appreciation Marketing is concerned, though, Narcissus is the guy who thinks the whole world revolves around him.

In the field of psychology, excessive narcissism is recognized as a severe personality dysfunction or personality disorder. The term *narcissistic* denotes vanity, conceit, egotism or simple selfishness. It is sometimes used to denote elitism or an indifference to the plight of others.

Again, we all know this creature.

I am the top producer in this area. *I* am number one in my office. *I* am this. *I* am that. Back in high school, they called this bragging. It's crucial that you avoid being pegged as Narcissus. Believe me, it doesn't look good on you.

I have an old friend who was a sales agent at a company I used to work for. He and I became friends as we grew our respective businesses into Europe. The foundation of our friendship was built on mutual respect. We continually spent long hours "comparing notes" and learning from one another.

We parted ways in business, but remained friends. He calls me about once a year to check in. During our phone calls, which are always short, he proceeds to tell me how much money he's making, what kind of car he's driving, what kind of house he's living in, and how much he stands to be making a year from now. He's always looking for another leader, and tells me I would be perfect for the job. He then makes a bunch of promises (all money related) on what will happen if I join him in his new venture.

Never once does he ask about my family, or my personal life.

Never once does he bring up mutual friends or attempt to reminisce about the old days.

Instead, he eventually gets around to asking how I'm doing in hope that I'll say "not so good." When I tell him that I'm doing phenomenally well, and although I'm super happy for him and all the success he's enjoying, I'm not personally interested in working with him . . . he suddenly has to get going.

The phone call has been the same five years in a row, and it won't change this year either. This friend is the classic example of Narcissus. He just doesn't get it.

Narcissus is an advanced case of The Topper. We classified The Topper in the "harmless but annoying" category (like those pigeons). Narcissus is the more flagrant version, maybe like the bull dog with the big spiked collar. "Look at me, everybody! I'm the big dog!"

It's important to point out that Narcissus isn't guilty only by the words he uses. It's in his actions, his expressions, his gestures, and the way he treats other people that make you just want to walk up and punch him in the face! Narcissus is usually glancing around the room during your conversation with him.

Back in my early days of playing baseball, I overheard one of the veterans on my team talking to one of the outspoken players who was always telling everybody how great he was. He said, "If you really are something special, you won't need to tell people. They'll figure it out on their own. And if they don't, other people will tell them for you." That statement stuck with me forever.

The Appreciator

. . . is Humble

Nobody wants to sit down with you and hear about how great and successful you are. It's okay to talk about your victories and tell your success stories. Just do it with humility. There's a fine line between arrogance and confidence. If you're confident, people will be drawn towards you. If you're arrogant they'll run the other way.

Learn to shift the focus from yourself to others. Try, instead, to find out about them and how great they are.

Make a practice of lifting up other people all day long. Tell people they look nice. Tell people what qualities about them you admire. Tell people you appreciate them.

The Vulture

It's difficult to pick The Vulture out of a crowd without eavesdropping on other peoples' conversations. In fact, although their population is expansive and they are indigenous to all climates and geographical areas, you usually don't spot The Vulture until you're sitting down with him.

You see, from ground level, The Vulture can look like a beautiful bird. They're sometimes mistaken for the majestic eagles and hawks of the world. But once you get right up close, The Vulture can be appalling, even hideous! And by then it's too late.

The Vulture is an aggressive bird of prey who arranges an appointment or a meeting with you under false pretenses. Normally, The Vulture is appearing interested in your goods or services or personality, but is clearly there to "turn the tables."

My friend Tony was recently contacted by a woman who lives out of state nearly three hours away by car. This woman called him on the phone and explained how she had heard wonderful things about him. She admired how he worked with people and had been able to build a strong professional network through appreciation. She wanted to meet with him, learn his secrets, and hear about his business. Tony agreed.

This woman made the long drive and when the two of them sat down, at a coffee shop, she unfurled her big nasty vulture wings! And it wasn't pretty. Turns out, she was a sales rep for an international sales company and was only interested in recruiting Tony to come and work for her. While she was genuinely interested in Tony's personality, his network, and his leadership ability she was only interested in it for her own personal gain. Tony could only laugh (since *he* wasn't the one who made the drive)! This woman actually talked to Tony for over two hours and never once asked him about himself or his business.

Beware The Vulture!

The Appreciator

. . . is Genuine and Patient

Just don't do this!! Think of yourself in a boat out on a lake. It's early in the morning and you're fishing. You see a school of fish right below the boat so you take your hook, you stand up in the boat, and you SLAM the hook down into the water in the spot where the fish are. What happens to the fish? Do you catch them all? Do you catch any? Actually chances are the fish are long gone before the hook breaks the surface. And guess what? They're not coming back! Cast your line out there, sit back, and reel it back in. Not to compare people to fish . . . but you can be sure that you won't see any people schooling up anywhere near The Vulture.

Mr. Halitosis

To be politically correct here, Mr. Halitosis can just as well be Mrs. or Ms. Halitosis. While the moniker calls to mind that person whose breath could melt the skin right off of your face—again, you know him—Mr. Halitosis isn't just the creature with the bad breath. He's the creature with the bad breath, the cat fur on his coat, the sloppy clothes, the messy hair, hmm maybe even some B.O. And if the offensive appearance isn't bad enough, Mr. Halitosis also gets right up into your personal space.

In addition to poor hygiene, Mr. Halitosis has poor social skills, no manners, and isn't respectful of others.

He might be a friend of yours. Maybe even a good friend. But he's not the person you'd invite to a dinner party or an important business function. You might be able to put up with Mr. Halitosis on a one-on-one basis, but you definitely go out of your way to keep him away from your friends. Mr. Halitosis will struggle to be successful in a business that deals with other people. He's better suited to be a toll booth operator in Antarctica. Be very careful that this section doesn't describe you.

"Mirror, mirror, on the wall; who's the problem after all?"

The mirror never lies.

The Appreciator

. . . is Clean

Simple question; would you do business with you?

Personal hygiene is a part of your likeability factor, and is important especially when making a first impression. Take a look at yourself and ask if you are physically pleasing to be around. We're not talking about having plastic surgery or becoming a pinup model, we're talking about being professional and clean. You don't have to become something you're not, just get better. And, while Mr. Halitosis was just a metaphor, breath mints and deodorant spray are a networker's best friend.

We poked a little bit of fun in this chapter, but let me reiterate that I have personally been some of these creatures in my lifetime. In fact, I'm sure I've—at one time or another—been all seven! Personal development is an integral part of everyone's evolution and this chapter is just a simple reminder that you must always be looking for ways to improve.

People go to war and lay down their lives for your right to be any one of these "creatures."

But they probably wouldn't refer you business.

CHAPTER FIVE

Chocolate Frosted Dog Crap

"The great enemy of clear language is insincerity."
—*George Orwell*

Now there's a pleasant thought!

Seriously, what if somebody scooped up a big pile of dog crap off the sidewalk and put it on a dessert plate? Next, they crafted it into a rounded shape and then covered it with chocolate frosting and stuck a candle in the middle. Finally, they sing Happy Birthday and set it down in front of you.

Is it a cake?

It *looks* like a cake. Even in the birthday pictures. But we have other senses that tip us off as to its real identity; namely, the smell. No matter what pretty decorations are used to disguise it, we have the ability (ten times out of ten) to "sniff it out" as what it really is . . . a pile of dog crap!

Now, from a business standpoint, do you think it would be beneficial to you and your business to present a person with a cake made of dog crap? It doesn't matter if it's a customer, a client, a perspective client, or a total stranger. If you give me a cake made of dog crap, I'll know it immediately and I will not like it. It will not endear you to me, and it will *not* result in my doing business with you.

There isn't a business person alive who will argue that point, yet people still do it (and spend large amounts of money to do it) every single day. Do we have your attention?

Let's explain the metaphor, which was indelibly etched into my consciousness by my friend Jordan Adler, author of *Beach Money*.

In this case, the chocolate frosted dog crap is simply a self-serving action that is being "dressed up" or disguised to look like a heartfelt gesture.

For example, when was the last time you received a phone call from somebody you hadn't heard from in a very long time? Your wheels immediately start turning, as to *why* you're receiving this phone call. Because it's not a person who normally calls you (or in this case, somebody you haven't heard from in a long time) your natural instinct is to put up a guard. Even though the conversation is polite, you just can't stop thinking "what does this person want?"

Caller: "Hey John, how the heck are ya? It's Kevin!

You: "Kevin Jones?"

Caller: "Yeah, it's been a long time!"

You: "Wow, what have you been up to?"

Caller: "I've bounced around a lot over the last ten years and now I'm back in town. I thought I'd look you up."

You: "I'm glad you did. Wow, lots has happened since I last saw you. I'm married now and have two little girls. What about you, did you ever get married or start a family?"

Caller: "No, I'm still single. Hey, I'd love to see you again. Could you get free for a beer some night next week?"

You: "Sure. I can get out for an hour or two on Wednesday night. Remember The Lodge, over there on Main Street? How about there at 7 o'clock?"

Caller: "Yeah, that sounds great man. Hey, just for the heck of it, bring along a copy of your electric bill. I'm in that business now and I'm pretty sure I can beat what you're paying."

BAM!!!!

From across the room, this call was looking like chocolate cake. Even though you started out a little skeptical, as it got closer and closer, it was still looking like cake. And right before you actually "lifted your fork"—BAM—you caught the aroma full flush, right in the face!

Kevin didn't call you to catch up. Kevin didn't call you to see what you've been up to. Kevin called you because he wants you to buy your electricity from him. In fact, he's probably "smiling and dialing" his night away and you're just a name on his list.

Consequently, before 7 o'clock on Wednesday night arrives, you call Kevin and leave him a "something just came up" voicemail message. And when he tries to call you back, you don't pick up. Kevin is done. And he was oh so close!

That's just one example of trying to put chocolate frosting on dog crap. And that grin on your face right now represents your recognition of the fact that—in some form or another—you've probably done this too.

It doesn't have to be in the form of a phone call, either. It's very simply the act of doing something with the full intent of getting something in return.

Another example of chocolate frosted dog crap would be a birthday card, an anniversary card, or a holiday card with your business card inside. Don't send someone a birthday card and say: *Happy Birthday Samantha! I was just thinking of you and hope you have a fabulous day! You deserve it! . . .*

Oh, and by the way, the greatest compliment I can receive is a warm referral!

PEW! That's another stinker. You had it, right up until that last line. Think about it. Whatever it is that you do for a living, your friends and associates *already know what that is*. If you send them an ad for your business and try to "dress it up" as a birthday card, it will be "sniffed out," exposed as a thoughtless act, and tossed directly into the garbage can. You will have likely done more damage than good.

Conversely, if you were to send your friends, customers, and clients a real heartfelt birthday card (hmm, there's an interesting idea), and kept it as such, you'd be a genius.

Try this: *Happy Birthday, Samantha! I was just thinking of you and hope you have a fabulous day! You deserve it!*

The reaction on the other end would be, "Wow, that was really nice." Instead of pulling out the baggie and "disposing of your card properly," Samantha would probably actually save the card and even display it. People would come to visit and see the card out. Samantha would even be sure to let her family know that she received a card from you (her accountant) and didn't even get one from her own sisters! Yes, she knows that you are her accountant even though you didn't put your business card or phone number inside the birthday card. And now she loves you for it. Turns out, it was the only birthday card she received this year!

A little sincerity still goes a long way in this world. The concept is so "old school" that people, in their efforts to do things better, faster and more efficiently have drifted farther and farther away from what is logical.

Business people have gotten so clever with their marketing tools and ideas these days, haven't they? We've all received the email telling us we've won something, or qualified for something, and all we have to do is go to a website and download a file. We're not really that stupid.

I have an old friend who I haven't been close to in ten years. I send him and his family a holiday card every year and I also get one back. Theirs however, always has a business card in it. The only time I ever hear from him, in fact, is when he's trying to pitch me on his business and his online grocery store. As a matter of fact, as I'm typing this paragraph I just received an email from him saying "Don't Miss Out" in the subject line. I opened it, noticed that it wasn't sent to me personally (but everybody in his address book), and that it's the same ad for his company that he's emailed me 50 times before. I wasn't interested in it then, I'm not interested in it now, and I'm a little turned off that he'd keep sending this to me. Let me point out, I love this man and his whole family. But if he called me right now, I wouldn't answer his call. He's been "sniffed out."

It's also important to remember that most of us deal with our real mail the same way. We sort it out over the garbage can. We, in essence, are sniffing out all the dog crap before we even track it into the house.

"I hate to get my mail," said Chris Avcollie, an attorney and founder of Lincoln Legal Support in Waterbury, CT. "When I go through my mail it usually puts me in a lousy mood. There's seldom anything there that I want. It's refreshing when there's actually a piece of personal mail in there. But it doesn't happen often."

Globally recognized as "junk mail," it's the creative-looking newsletters and recipe cards and pre-qualifications and postcards and flyers and brochures that fill up our mailboxes and, ultimately, our waste baskets and landfills. How about those ads disguised as greeting cards where a total stranger is addressing you by your first name, and writing to you as though you are friends— telling you all about their product or service?

NONE OF IT GETS PAST THE GATE KEEPER! STOP IT!!!

As I type this chapter, it's the holiday season and I'm being flooded with holiday cards. I always love to receive holiday cards and it seems that every year we pin up more and more around the doorway into our family room.

This year, more than ever before, I'm paying attention to the energy attached to my holiday cards. I never really realized that I knew so many poop senders!

This one was a really nice thought, but it has the guy's business card inside. WHAT is he thinking? This one is from my lawn guy! What a GREAT touch! He actually just wishes me Happy Holidays with no poop-a-ganda! (new word!) This one is from the jewelry store in New York City where I bought my wife a ring ten years ago! He has sent one every year, which I've always admired. But, uh-oh, this year's has *coupons* inside!! WHAT??!! "Merry Christmas" would have done the trick! What's that smell? It's not holiday cookies!

If I came home tonight and saw three messages flashing on my voicemail—from all three of these people—guess which call I'd return? Yep, the lawn guy.

The next time you get your mail, or receive a sales call or a voice message, take a second to consider the sincerity of the "sender." Is this person genuinely interested in you as a human being? Or is he trying to present you with a pungent, fresh-baked pile of you-know- what?

Don't you make the same mistake.

The Appreciator

. . . is Sincere

If you must contact someone regarding business, then contact them regarding business. Don't try to disguise your business efforts as appreciation. They're not the same thing.

By the same token, if you are contacting someone as an act of appreciation, then make it 100% about that.

Remember, if you practice Appreciation Marketing principles, the people you are appreciating already know what you do for a living. You don't need to suggest it to them. If you are genuine, you are already on their mind in a positive way.

CHAPTER SIX

Plant a TOMATO Garden

"Cherish your human connections; your relationships with friends and family."

—*Barbara Bush*

Please allow me to qualify the title of this chapter by saying that I do *not* have a green thumb. I can't keep a house plant alive, let alone grow anything in a garden. I'm also of the mind that says, "Why would I bother growing tomatoes in a garden? If I want tomatoes, I'll drive down the street, walk into a supermarket and purchase some. This isn't 1855! It's not that difficult."

Now before I further offend any of you "work-from-home farmers," this chapter is about a different kind of tomato. Here, we're breaking down the acronym, TOMATO. It stands for "Top of Mind Awareness . . . *Through Others*."

Top of Mind Awareness (TOMA), is when somebody thinks of you whenever a certain topic comes up. Maybe you're a huge New York Yankees fan and all your friends and family know it. You wear a Yankee hat around town, you wear a team shirt once and a while, you're always going to games, and they're your favorite topic at parties. You're recognized, by all who know you, as "the biggest

Yankee fan I know." Whenever the Yankees come up, everybody you know instantly and automatically thinks of you.

As you can imagine, there's not a whole lot of benefit attached to that kind of TOMA.

But what if you're a Realtor? What if you sell mortgages, or insurance, or cars? What if you're a lawyer, a doctor, a dentist, a chiropractor, or a veterinarian? What if you own a car wash, a dry cleaning business, a karate studio, a deli, or a restaurant? Would it be valuable if every time a need for your product or service came up in conversation, somebody thought of you instantly and automatically? That's the kind of TOMA that every person desires, and it's what will result from practicing the principles in this book.

But how much business can you do exclusively through your friends and family? It might not even be enough to pay the bills. As great as it would be to have earned TOMA with your "circle of influence," the fact remains— we all know a finite number of people.

Psychology Today, a mainstream psychology magazine, stated that by the age of 21, everybody knows on average 2,000 people on a first name basis. If that research is true, then it suggests that you have at least 2,000 people you know, and who know you.

I don't want to question that research, but just in case you do, let's perform a little "reduction to the ridiculous" and instead assume that we all know only 200 people. No arguments there.

Now let's assume that you are a Master of Appreciation Marketing. You're a giver. You have been throughout your entire life. So not only do 200 people know you, but those 200 people actually *like* you as well. They think of you fondly (because you think of *them* fondly) and they always think of you when your product or service is mentioned. You are a Master.

Let's take it a step further and say that you are a Realtor. And let's say that the average person purchases a new house every six years.

If you have 200 people in your "circle," let's say that 150 are local and 50 are married couples. That leaves you with 100 people who are ready, willing, and able to sell their house through you when the time comes. If you sell houses for 100 people over six years, that would average out to 16 houses per year. Not too bad. And you were able to accomplish this without taking newspaper ads, or doing any advertising. You were able to make this happen because you are a Master.

But as good as that is, it's not enough. Your goal is to sell five homes per month, not 16 per year.

Enter TOMATO: (Top of Mind Awareness, *Through Others*).

Let's go back to our psychology stats.

If you have 200 people in your circle of influence, then that psychology magazine says that they each know 2,000. Again, let's scale that back and say that they (like you) know 200.

Question: If you know 200 people and those people know you, like you, and think of you fondly every time your product or service is mentioned, would it be a stretch to say that they'd refer you to the 200 people *they* know when your product or service comes up in *their* conversations? Please realize that if this occurred you would potentially have 40,000 people who may be interested in doing business with you because of the TOMATO garden that you cultivated. All because you made a decision to be a Master of Appreciation!

Forget the Realtor analogy for a minute. I'd challenge anybody in any profession to write 40,000 pieces of business per year. That would be 3,333 per month or 107 per day, working seven days a week. Hmmm. That is a good problem to have!

OK, so 40,000 people might seem a little far fetched. So let's scale it back even further. What if you took care of your 200 people and they each spread the good word to only the top 20 people in their networks. That would still result in 4,000 warm connections. Nice!

When I built my dream house in 1999, I moved in across the street from one of the most well-known Realtors in our town. It was a new town for me, so I had never heard of these people but I had seen their name all over town on "for sale" signs.

Upon moving in, they came down our long driveway, knocked on the front door, introduced themselves, and welcomed us to the neighborhood. And over the course of the next five years, we were invited to their house for parties three times a year. The whole town was there! When I stopped at their door with my little girl on Halloween, they'd offer me a drink to take with me during the rest of my trick-or-treat adventure. One time, the newspaper did a story on me and these neighbors cut it out, laminated it, and sent it to me with a congratulations message. These people were the first real Masters I had ever met.

During the housing boom a few years later, I decided to put my house on the market to see what I could get for it. I called my neighbors to list it for me.

Even though I had no fewer than a dozen friends who were Realtors, and even though these neighbors never asked me to do business with them, I just wanted to. It was TOMA at its finest!

Our friend Jordan Adler, author of *Beach Money*, is one of the most successful networkers in the world. He believes that there are three factors that will determine how powerful your network will be as it relates to your income and your success.

1. How many people do you have in your contact manager?

2. What is the quality of the relationships you have with the people in your contact manager? (Do they like you and do they trust you?)

3. Do those people in your contact manager remember you?

Jordan uses "dots" as an illustration of what happens when the three factors above are present.

If you make two dots on a piece of paper, how many lines can you draw connecting those dots? Not a trick question. You can draw just one. There is one connection between two dots.

Now how many connections are there between three dots? There are three. By adding just one more dot; you added two more lines or connections.

When you add just one more dot (a fourth), you will add another three connections for a total of six.

Take it just one more step and add a fifth dot. Now your connections go from six to ten.

Now let's pretend that each dot represents a person. As you add people to your network and enhance the relationship that they have with you (and each other) your number of relationships increases exponentially.

"I meet people that seem to have all the luck," Jordan says. "Great things seem to happen to them all the time. What I have learned is that I can actually increase the chances that amazing things will happen to me every day. And anybody can do the same thing by simply increasing the number of *quality* contacts in their circle of influence and then doing their best to make sure many of them know each other. What appears to be a miracle or coincidence may actually be a function of the number of possibilities created by the size of your network."

I've watched Jordan Adler's TOMATO garden grow consistently—on a daily basis—simply because of his attitude towards other people.

The bottom line is that the Law of Appreciation Marketing has a trickle down effect. And it always trickles back up to you when you recognize the people within your "circle of influence" as unique human beings. Tell them and *show* them that you appreciate them. You'll never have to ask for business again.

A close friend of mine is the founder and CEO of his own company that specializes in appreciating, and finding the good in people. He says, *"Don't ask for the referral. Deserve it."* To expand on his sentiment, *"Don't just say something nice about somebody. Mean it."*

The Appreciator

. . . Builds Strong Relationships

You wouldn't take seeds, scatter them on blacktop, and hope something grows. So don't do it in your business and personal life that way either.

Any person can start a TOMATO garden today. Simply contact someone and begin a relationship (personal or professional). Spend time watering and nurturing that relationship.

Make this a daily habit within your Appreciation Marketing Strategy, and then you'll be able to sit back and watch your garden grow.

CHAPTER SEVEN

Serve Others

"It is one of the most beautiful compensations of life that no man can sincerely try to help another without helping himself."

—*Ralph Waldo Emerson*

I can't help thinking back to a 1950's Twilight Zone rerun where aliens came down from outer space causing panic and global chaos. They couldn't communicate with the Earthlings, but order was restored when the government was able to decode the title of a large book their leader was carrying. It was called *How to Serve Man*.

It wasn't until the end of the show that they decoded the rest of the writing and discovered that it was a cookbook!

An excellent way to go about your new Appreciation Marketing Strategy would be to focus on serving others. Not for dinner, but by finding ways to help them achieve their goals and dreams.

If you were running for any elected office, for example, your objective would be to get out into the community and build relationships. You'd want to create top of mind awareness, so that people wouldn't have to actually "think" when they went into the voting booth to pull the lever. They vote for you because they feel like you're their friend. They feel like you *serve them.*

To accomplish this, political campaigns center around meeting as many people as possible, shaking hands, kissing babies, but most importantly, finding out what these people *want* and formulating a plan to help them get it (e.g., campaign promises). If my problem is health care and you promise to help solve my problem—then guess what? I'm voting for you. And not only am I voting for you, I'm going to convince all my friends and colleagues that they should vote for you as well. In fact, I'm even going to put your name on a bumper sticker and drive around with it on the back of my car! I may even put a sign on my front lawn, declaring my allegiance!

I've always thought it curious, how people get so passionate in backing their politicians. It all goes back to what the great Zig Ziglar says about success in anything; "You can have everything *you* want, if you just help enough other people get what *they* want." Isn't that a remarkable concept?

During the writing of this book, Barack Obama made history as he was elected the first black president of the United States. During the campaign I saw so many negative emails flying around about Obama. People said he was associating with terrorists, he refused to say the Pledge of Allegiance, he took the American flag off his private jet, he was dishonest, etc. Those are some pretty harsh criticisms. Yet Obama won the election by a wide margin. It's because his personality was appealing to people; but more importantly, his message *"Change"* promised to help people get what they wanted. In the midst of a recession, and one of the worst economies in decades, people wanted change. Obama's message served them.

So how does this relate to your business? You probably aren't running for office, and you probably don't have hundreds of millions of dollars to campaign for your business. So start at the grass roots level.

Let's say that you and I meet at a networking function. You tell me that you sell mortgages, and I tell you that I'm a landscaper. You then proceed to ask me what rate I'm paying on my mortgage and offer to buy me a cup of coffee to discus saving me some money.

In this scenario, are you attempting to help me get what I want? The sad thing is, you think "yes." In your deluded mind, you think that you're trying to "help me" by getting me a lower mortgage rate. But the truth is, you're trying to "help" yourself. You're trying to *get* business.

What's going to happen? I'll meet you for coffee and listen to your mortgage pitch, all the while trying to find a way to switch the conversation over to landscaping. I have zero interest in refinancing and you have zero interest in hiring me to cut your grass. So, in essence, we're both wasting valuable time in what most likely will end in a stalemate. We'll leave the meeting with each others' business cards and no intention of ever calling the other guy back.

How about this instead?

You and I meet at the networking event. Instead of you telling me what you do, you ask me what *I* do. I then proceed to tell you that I'm a landscaper. You reply, "I have a large and growing network in this area and I might be able to be a good referral source for you. Let's have a cup of coffee and you can tell me more about what you do, and how I might be able to help."

How do you suppose someone might respond to that?

For starters, after accepting your offer enthusiastically, my next question would be, "what do *you* do?" Then in the hours or days leading up to our coffee appointment, I'd be thinking of potential referrals for you, so that I won't feel uncomfortable only being on the receiving end.

The big kicker here is, that you then have to make good on your offer. Don't just say it and then show up for coffee with guns-a-blazin' talking about the mortgage industry.

Is it really that difficult to be interested in other people? Really find out what I do as a landscaper. Maybe, in addition to cutting lawns, I also do plantings, mulch, spring and fall cleanup, plow snow, and build stone walls. Maybe you uncover that I do something that you need. And if not you, maybe somebody you know is looking. If, instead of trying to convince me to refinance my mortgage, you refer me some potential business, what do you suppose my reaction would be?

Yes—to reciprocate.

In one of the most famous speeches of all time, U.S. President John F. Kennedy said, *"And so, my fellow Americans, ask not what your country can do for you; ask what you can do for your country."* Learn a lesson from JFK. "Ask not" what other people can do for you; ask what you can do for them.

Deepak Chopra, in his book *The Seven Spiritual Laws of Success* says:

> *If you want joy, give joy to others; if you want love, learn to give love; if you want attention and apprecia- tion, learn to give attention and appreciation; if you want material affluence, help others to become materi- ally affluent. In fact, the easiest way to get what you want is to help others get what they want. This princi- ple works equally well for individuals, corporations, societies, and nations. If you want to be blessed with all the good things in life, learn to silently bless every- one with all the good things in life.*

Caring about other people and taking a genuine interest in them is also part of your forming a magnetic personal- ity. And isn't that what you'd like where your business and personal life are concerned?

Imagine how successful you'd be if you were the kind of person (unlike the creatures in Chapter Four) who attracted people effortlessly wherever you went?

Let's take Curtis. He was the captain and shortstop for the baseball team at Division I, Sacred Heart University and was studying for a degree in Business Management. If you had told Curtis that upon his graduation he'd spend two years walking into companies selling floor mats and toilet paper he might have laughed in your face.

"Most people don't understand that the Law of Attraction isn't just about attracting things into your life," he says. "It also applies to the types of people you attract."

Curtis remembers getting dressed up and putting on his confident swagger for a career fair his school was hosting. He walked in there looking to bag a sexy job with Smith Barney, UBS, or Merrill Lynch.

"What really struck me," he said, "was that the majority of the recruiters at the booths for those companies were not all that warm and friendly. They mostly looked cold and constipated. At one booth, though, I was stopped and greeted by a man with a big handshake and an even bigger smile. I instantly liked this guy. I had no idea what his company was all about, but his magnetic personality is what sold me on an interview. I made the decision to go to work for that company for two reasons. The most important reason was because I liked Jon Cohen."

Without knowing it, Jon Cohen became a teacher and role model to Curtis Lewsey, and an inspiration for this book. Coincidentally, he's a huge success as a sales manager for Cintas Corporation.

Curtis went with Cintas because Cohen had a magnetic personality. Why? Because Jon Cohen understood the principles of Appreciation Marketing.

I've often found it curious that the top sales professionals and the topnotch sales-training gurus practice what they call the "ABCs of Sales." In their world, ABC stands for "Always Be Closing." Not to fly in the face of years of sales wisdom, but I've always gotten by on the ABCs of Appreciation. In my world its *"Always Be Charming."*

The Appreciator

. . . Is a Giver

The best thing you can do to be the type of person that other people want to be around, and do business with, is to become an expert at building rapport. Anthony Robbins is a master of using Neuro-Linguistic Programming to accomplish this. Start by finding commonality between yourself and another person. Appreciate the fact that you have a common interest and share a story that applies. Give sincere compliments and become a sincere acceptor of compliments as well. Ask people questions about themselves and listen. Ask them about the things they like to do and what their desires are.

If you can genuinely care about somebody else, then it's easy to pass them referrals and you can count on them returning the favor.

CHAPTER EIGHT

Card Collecting

"Referrals come through who you are, not what you sell."

—*Bill Cates*

As a kid I was a passionate collector of baseball cards. When I started out, they were a nickel a pack, then a dime, a quarter, and finally fifty cents. I haven't purchased a pack in thirty years, but I think they're up to around five bucks now!

I'd sort those cards on my bedroom floor for hours until my neck and back were locked in a hunch position. I'd know exactly how many Reggie Jackson cards I had, in each season, and I'd get on the phone with my friends and work out trades to get the players I needed to complete each set. My goal, always, was to collect every player from each season.

I had a special box that had a slot for each team. American League on one side, and National League on the other. Nothing was more exciting to me than sitting down with twenty new packs of baseball cards, slowly opening each one, slamming the pink cardboard-like gum into my mouth and chomping until my jaw was sore. There was a feeling of elation when I'd open up a pack containing a star player or a card I needed to complete a team. And the "doubles" and "triples" would fall into a separate pile for trading when I got to school the next morning.

I was able to collect every league set, every year, without fail. One of the reasons for this was, in addition to being passionate about what I was doing, I wasn't doing it to try and make money. I was doing it for fun to complete a task. If I needed a Tom Seaver card to complete a set and my friend needed a Johnny Nobody card to complete his, he'd have no reservations about trading me his extra Seaver for my extra Nobody. If it had been about making money, this could never and would never have happened. Not unless I had real dumb friends.

Now that I have you thoroughly confused, I'm not really suggesting that you start an actual baseball card collection.

But what if you attended networking events twice a week, and made it a goal to collect *business cards*? What if, with the same passion I just described for baseball cards, you collected business cards?

Since adopting Appreciation Marketing principles in early 2007, my partner and I have collected over 3,000 business cards. These cards aren't in a shoebox, a drawer, or a pile. They're in plastic notebook pages, just like baseball cards, sorted strategically according to where we met, what groups they belong to, and what they do. If you ask me about a painter, I have ten. If you need somebody to mow your lawn, I have ten. I have Realtors, mortgage brokers, financial planners . . . what do you need?

"You need a Tom Seaver? Well, I've got one right here for you!"

Going back to our coffee appointment example, how might your business be enhanced if you made it a point to meet people, get their business cards, and create sincere "giving" relationships? What if you made it a point to refer business to people and expected nothing in return? I'm going to suggest that you'll have other people referring you more business than you can handle.

"If I had to name the single characteristic shared by all the truly successful people I've met in my lifetime, I'd have to say it's the ability to create and nurture a network of contacts," wrote Harvey Mackay in his book, *The Rolodex Network Builder*.

Another friend of ours, Bill Cates, president of Referral Coach International and author of *Unlimited Referrals; Secrets That Turn Business Relationships Into Gold*, calls these types of business relationships "referral alliances."

"I know some salespeople who have built incredible careers using this referral alliance strategy," he said. "Just as referral selling is more than just a bunch of techniques (it's a way of thinking), so too is this concept of forming referral alliances. You move through life acting on the knowledge that building strong, mutually beneficial relationships with people, even those who may never buy what you sell, will take you to higher levels of success."

And don't just take Harvey and Bill's word for it.

Dr. Ivan Misner founded an entire global company based on these very principles. Business Networking International (BNI) has grown to become the world's largest and most successful business networking organization with thousands of chapters, all over the world.

The motto of BNI is "Givers Gain."

"The central, guiding philosophy of BNI has always been the concept of giving benefit to others," Dr. Misner said in his book, *Givers Gain*. "It's an ethical theme that is common to all religions, all cultures; treat others the way you want to be treated. If you want to get referrals, do the best job you can of giving referrals to others.

"Marketing is sometimes approached as a sort of big-game hunt. The customers are out there in the woods; you have to load up with your best ads and promotional materials and seek them out, one by one. If you're a good shot, you get instant satisfaction. The more you bag, the better your business—but it's hard work, and you can never rest. You have to go out every day and find more big game."

"Building a business through referral networking is more like farming. Unlike hunting, you don't expect instant returns. Instead, you cultivate relationships by offering others referrals, expert assistance, and other benefits. You form long-lasting referral partnerships based on trust. And if you are steadfast and patient, your efforts will pay off and you will reap a bountiful harvest: business opportunities that your networking partners refer to you."

The Law of Attraction states that "what you give out is what you'll get back." Become a "connector" and put other people first. The result will be a life of abundance—not only in your professional life, but in your personal life as well. And, as Jordan Adler explained in Chapter 6, for every "dot" you add, the results are exponential.

Another way to look at this is how to remain ahead of the curve as a professional in the "shipping business." It doesn't matter what you do for a living. To paraphrase John Milton Fogg, one of the true masters of networking, we're all in the shipping and receiving business. That's relation*shipping*, partner*shipping*, leader*shipping* and friend*shipping*. The better you are at the "shipping" side of the equation, the more "receiving" you will enjoy.

The Appreciator

. . . is a Connector

Start your very own Business Card Collection! Don't just pluck them off bulletin boards and countertops though. Actually make it part of your Appreciation Marketing Strategy to meet at least one new person every day and collect their business card. After doing so, send them an email telling them it was nice to meet them (if it was), send them a personal note or greeting card saying the same, add them to your contact management system, and file their business card in such a way that you can easily recall it. Make it a point to stay in touch with this person. Remember, the card isn't a card. It represents a human being.

Watch your collection grow and sincerely try to connect these people with other people who might be a good fit for them both personally and professionally.

A great mantra to practice is "Two a day will bring freedom my way."

CHAPTER NINE

That Little Extra

"The difference between ordinary and extraordinary is that little extra."

> —*Fomer Dallas Cowboys coach, Jimmy Johnson*

In their book *212 The Extra Degree*, Sam Parker and Mac Anderson point out the fact that at 211-degrees, water is hot. At 212-degrees it boils. With boiling water comes steam, and steam can power a locomotive. They point out that "it's the one extra degree of effort, in business and in life, that can separate the good from the great."

The goal of this chapter is not to preach to you about going the extra mile to become better at what you do. That's the goal of *their* book. Our objective is to get you to be an extra miler when it comes to your Appreciation Marketing Strategy.

What does that mean?

It's inconvenient to go out of your way to recognize and appreciate people all day long. Even if it's your full-time job, it's a challenging task. It's time consuming.

You have so many email messages to sort through and reply to, so many phone calls to return, errands to run, tasks to accomplish. How in the world can you find the time to call somebody on the phone just to tell them you're thinking about them? How can you take the time to write out greeting cards and actually mail them? Where in the world can you find the time to meet people for coffee or lunch?

The answer lies in these ten two-letter words: *"if it is to be, it is up to me."* You don't *have* to do these things. Nobody will make you. In fact, your competition would prefer that you don't! Have you ever heard the adage, *"If you don't take care of your customers, somebody else will?"* Well, it's the truth. And it holds true for your customers, your friends, your family, and even your spouse. *"If you don't appreciate your people, somebody else will."* And when they do, you lose.

Sales statistics on "why customers leave" show that one out of a hundred will die, three will relocate, five will buy from a friend, nine will be stolen by a competitor, fourteen will leave on price point, and sixty eight out of a hundred will leave you because of perceived indifference.

What, exactly, is perceived indifference? Well, let's think about it a minute. Perceived indifference could mean that your customer didn't think you'd care if he left. Or, it could mean that he didn't think you cared about him. Or maybe he doesn't care about you.

Whatever it actually means, one thing is for sure . . .

A customer will *stay* if they think you *do* care about them! And if they think you care about them . . . they care about you.

Implementing this Appreciation Marketing Strategy isn't as daunting a task as you might think. Start small. Craft your list and fill it with every person you know or have known. Start with your circle of influence which starts with friends, family, associates (basically anyone you might invite to your wedding), and goes on to include anyone you might nod to or say hello to if you ran into them in aisle six at the grocery store.

Next, use memory joggers like the yellow pages. Think of schools and churches you attend or used to attend. Think of activities you enjoy and clubs you belong to or have belonged to. Go through your old stack of business cards.

These are the initial people to whom your appreciation should flow. Start out with the obvious, your family. Maybe make a habit of just one quick phone call a day. Something like *"Hi Richie, I don't have a lot of time to chat, but I was thinking of you on my ride into work this morning and I just felt prompted to give you a quick shout and see how you're doing. That's great. Hey, have a great day. Let's try to get together again soon."*

That wasn't tough. Let's call it five minutes, max.

Next, how about grabbing a stack of thank you cards, a stack of nice-to-meet-you cards, and a few birthday cards and keep them in a box in your office, along with a roll of stamps. How about once or twice a day, you pull one out, tell somebody that you're thinking about them, address the envelope and put it in the mailbox.

We'll call that ten to fifteen minutes (make it an hour if you include stopping at the store for the supplies). Now you're up to 20 minutes a day, or at the most one hour.

Smiles, hugs, handshakes and kind words don't need to have time budgeted, as they just come during the natural course of your day.

Now the killer question . . . Is it worth just a few minutes a day to build stronger personal and professional relationships in your life? If the answer to that question is "no," then you can use the rest of this book to line your bird cage. If it's "yes," then *what's stopping you?*

Oh, an hour is a long time in your busy world? Wake up 15 minutes earlier, go to lunch 15 minutes later, get back from lunch 15 minutes earlier, and go to bed 15 minutes later. There's your hour.

Robin M. Hensley, author of *Raising the Bar*, is a business development coach specializing in coaching attorneys and CPAs who are at the top of their game, to maximize their rainmaking skills. She has built a career out of not only being an Extra-Miler, but she teaches her clients these same principles as well.

"I look for excuses to send people notes on a daily basis," said Hensley, who was recognized by the *Atlanta Business Chronicle* as one of *Atlanta's Top 20 Self-Made Women*. "If I see someone at a conference and can't get across the room to speak with them, I'll send them a note to say, 'I'm sorry we didn't get a chance to speak. Let's have lunch.' "

Ms. Hensley believes that taking the extra few minutes to send an actual greeting card, as opposed to just an email, sets her apart and shows someone that she recognizes them as a human being. "A written note also shows that you're a very thoughtful and organized person."

As an insightful entrepreneur, Ms. Hensley also sends her clients Thanksgiving cards instead of the typical holiday cards in December. And instead of sending a stock card with her company name—in bulk—she's sure to use a personal greeting on each card individually. "I often get calls from clients to thank me," she said. "One client in particular actually framed a congratulatory card I sent him and hung it on his office wall. People are amazed that you are interested in their personal lives."

Clearly, she practices all of the Appreciation principles, and Ms. Hensley is confident that sending cards with personal notes has been heavily responsible in her success. "People know when you're sincere in your intent," she said. "It's not a marketing tool and it's not a matter of just going through the motions. My business is about people and helping them achieve their goals. When you write to recognize people for their accomplishments, it makes them feel better and also makes you feel better."

Appreciation principles, while they will make your business life light up, are as important, if not more important, in your personal life. So often we take for granted the people who are closest to us.

For example, if we spend all day recognizing and appreciating our business associates—and even total strangers—and then come home and yell at our spouses and children, we're missing the point. Don't make it a habit to recognize all your clients on their birthdays and then forget your own family members.

Appreciation isn't a to-do list. It needs to be a principle. It needs to be a habit. It needs to be carried out at a level of unconscious competence.

The Appreciator

. . . Goes the Extra Mile

There are many ways to set yourself apart and apply that "little extra." There's no replacement for the handwritten note or handwritten greeting card. However, to implement an Appreciation Marketing Strategy that calls for multiple notes and cards every day, this could become logistically impossible for a busy professional.

Curtis and I use an online service called SendOutCards which we have found to be the perfect mechanism to apply all of our appreciation principles.

Not only does SendOutCards allow you to send someone an actual greeting card in your own handwriting and with your own signature and personal photos in just seconds, it also allows you to send people gifts along with the cards, all with the ease and simplicity of a few mouse clicks. It also comes with a contact management system that keeps track of birthdays, anniversaries, and other important dates.

There are other systems out there, so find the one that works best for you.

Now you have the tools to become an Extra Miler.

CHAPTER TEN

Breakfast of Champions

"Man is fond of counting his troubles, but he does not count his joys. If he counted them up as he ought to, he would see that every lot has enough happiness provided for it."

— *Fyodor Dostoyevsky*

N o, not Wheaties.

Let me explain the scene when I woke up this morning.

My wife and my oldest daughter had been out of town all week, visiting relatives in California. My three-year-old daughter Cassidy and I had been sleeping together in daddy's bed. It was 20-degrees outside and the entire yard was covered by a solid sheet of ice on top of four or five inches of snow.

It was Friday morning, a work day for most, but neither an alarm clock's buzz nor a single fleeting though of responsibility disturbed that wonderful feeling of being toasty warm under the comforter in an otherwise chilly bedroom.

As I heard the faint sound of the telephone ringing in my office downstairs I opened my eyes and noticed the clock on the television cable box said 9:20. "Nice!" I thought to myself. "Cassidy never sleeps this late. I'm not moving!"

With no plans to go back to sleep, I just laid there and looked at my sleeping angel, all cozy under the blanket. We had left the gas fireplace on all night and I just stared into the fire for a while and let my mind run wild.

Suddenly thoughts of extreme gratitude came over me; More so than usual. "How many people," I wondered, "can just oversleep without panic on a random weekday? How many people live in a beautiful home with a fireplace in the master bedroom? How many people are blessed to have a beautiful spouse and two beautiful and healthy children? Even our yellow lab, Buttercup, has it better than most people. Just look at her curled up with her own fur blanket at the foot of the bed! How many people can say that they love their lives? Seriously, I love everything about my life!" The thoughts went on and on.

Then it occurred to me, that this was an amazing way to start off a day! I can't remember another time when I woke up and felt as personally fulfilled before ever getting out of bed. And while certainly many people don't enjoy the same luxuries as I do, and many others enjoy far more, clearly every person alive has so much to be grateful for if they'd just "wake up and smell the coffee."

It was just this morning that I had adopted a brand new philosophy. From now on, I will give myself Appreciation for Breakfast. How might your outlook on life improve if you just spent five minutes in the morning looking around and reflecting on all you're grateful for in your life. Just dream up a rambling punch list of everything that makes you happy. The negative stuff isn't allowed in; just the good stuff.

We've heard it said many times before that we are blessed with the most amazing computer ever invented. It's called our brain. This brain, like a computer, runs on a program. That means it can only produce output based on the input that we feed into it.

Long ago I learned to write down my goals and read them before retiring to bed at night. I've made this a habit for ten years and, though I don't do it every night, I can honestly say that I sleep much better and dream much better dreams than most people in the world. I've heard it said that the last thing that goes into your head before you go to sleep is what affects how you sleep, what you dream, and how you wake up the next day.

On that note, most people watch the 11 o'clock death and destruction report on television before nodding off. It's no wonder we're surrounded by such negativity in our lives.

To implement a solid Appreciation Marketing Strategy, why not take the goal setting practice to a higher level? In addition to reading and ingesting your goals before you go to sleep, why not run through them one more time before you start your day?

Recognizing and appreciating the blessings in your life make a healthier breakfast than anything else you can find on a menu. And we can all come up with multiple reasons to be grateful and appreciative.

So take a helping of that with your pancakes, and start your day with appreciation for breakfast. Watch what happens next!

The Appreciator

. . . Recognizes His Assets

Go ahead, get started right now.

What are some ways that you can start your day with appreciation? What things are most dear to your life? See that? You really are lucky. Go ahead and write a list. When you get it down on paper it becomes much more real. It will also lead you to other things to be grateful for.

CHAPTER ELEVEN

The Answer to Your Prayers

"When you are grateful fear disappears and abundance appears."

—Anthony Robbins

Iwas raised in the Catholic faith, but it doesn't make any difference what your religion is. Even those of us who don't practice any religion at all have, at one time or another, asked for a little "divine intervention."

Maybe it was on the roulette wheel. "Oooo, *please*, one time! Come on, number fifteen! Papa needs a new pair of shoes!"

Maybe while watching the big football game. "PLEASE! Just this once! Just one touchdown! I'll never ask for anything else!"

You might have been getting ready for your big outdoor wedding. "Oh, please! Just make it a sunny day. Please, I don't care if it rains for forty straight days after that. Just make it sunny tomorrow!"

We also pray a lot in business. "Please let me close this one big deal."

"Please don't let my boss find out."

"Please don't let this stock tank."

Perhaps your reasons are less superficial. "Please, keep my family safe through this horrible storm." Or, "please help my mother recover from this awful sickness." Even, "please help *me* through this difficult time."

Did you ever think it odd that when people pray, consciously or otherwise, they always seem to be *asking* for something? They only seem to pray in a time of need. Well, doesn't it stand to reason that the laws of appreciation—which I submit are universal laws—should then also hold up when it comes to praying?

A few years back I was watching a television show in which the quarterback of a high school football team suffered a devastating spinal injury and was carted off the field on a stretcher. This kid was a huge high school star and was on his way to a major college program and, ultimately, a professional career.

The next scene took place in the hospital room with the boy completely immobilized and his family all gathered around his bed. The doctor entered the room and broke the news that the young man was paralyzed from the waist down and it was doubtful that he'd ever walk again. He certainly would never play football again.

Later that night, his cheerleader girlfriend by his bedside, the young man broke down and began to cry. His girlfriend, comforting him, took his hand and began to pray aloud:

Lord we thank you for helping Billy get through this terrible accident. We thank you for the family and friends who are in his corner, and for giving him the strength to get through whatever lies ahead. We don't know what it is yet, but we know you have a plan and that you never give a person more difficulty than they can handle. We thank you for all the blessings in our lives, and we promise to never let you down.

Does that sound like the prayer of a person who just lost so much? The girl in the scene wasn't asking for any divine intervention. She was being appreciative for what she, and her boyfriend, already had. She was saying thank you!

The scene from that show made a tremendous impact on my life and the way I think. It teaches a profound lesson about life. Be thankful. Be appreciative. Recognize and acknowledge the things in your life that you have.

In his best-selling book, *The Science of Getting Rich,* written way back at the turn of the last century, Wallace Wattles wrote:

The moment you permit your mind to dwell with dissatisfaction upon things as they are, you begin to lose ground. You fix attention upon the common, the poor, the squalid, and the mean—and your mind takes the form of those things. You will then transmit these forms or mental images to the formless. Thus, the common, the poor, the squalid, and the mean will come to you. To permit your mind to dwell upon the inferior is to become inferior and to surround yourself with inferior things. On the other hand, to fix your attention on the best is to surround yourself with the best and to become the best.

Wattles is saying that you simply need to make the choice.

"The grateful mind," he adds, "is constantly fixed upon the best. Therefore, it tends to become the best; it takes the form or character of the best and will receive the best."

Reasons to be grateful are all around us, even in the worst of times. Yet, it is so easy to take these things for granted.

Jim Jacobus, CEO of 'A' Players Only!, has more than twenty years of research and application in human behavior and performance. He has also held the designation of being the #1 trainer worldwide with America's largest seminar company. Jim Jacobus has long understood the importance of appreciation and gratitude. "I have prayed many prayers in my life," he said. "I, like many, have prayed that God would do something for me, get me out of trouble or give me something I want. Over time my prayers have changed.

"A few months back a good friend of mine had his son diagnosed with a very difficult, life changing disease," he said. "Then his youngest son was diagnosed with the same disease, and then his oldest daughter. I was questioning him on how he and his wife were handling things and he told me they had adopted a new 'approach to prayer'. He told me that he had learned not to pray for a lighter load but instead to pray for a stronger back!

"I am adopting the same approach. Rather than wish for an easier life, I am praying for a back strong enough to appreciate all that comes my way, that my life would be full, and that I might actually live life every day I am blessed to be alive!"

The Appreciator

. . . is Grateful

If you're somebody who prays, try this in a prayer. If you don't pray, then try it as a toast. But take a second and verbally express thanks for the blessings in your life. An attitude of appreciation trumps out on an attitude of entitlement. Just a quick change in that belief pattern will allow you to move in a more positive direction.

William James, a pioneering American psychologist in the late 1800's, said, "The greatest revolution of our generation is the discovery that human beings, by changing the inner attitudes of their minds, can change the outer aspects of their lives."

It all starts with a conscious decision on your end.

CHAPTER TWELVE

It's Always Sunny
Above the Clouds

*"I wept because I had no shoes, until I met a man
who had no feet."*

—*Ancient Persian saying*

Sitting in the airport in Houston, tired from running an all-day seminar the day before and staying out late for an over-the-top Texas steak dinner, Curtis and I were dragging as we looked out the window at the dark, rainy, overcast morning. We got on the plane, got as comfortable as possible, and spent some time reflecting on our first-ever law of attraction workshop, which had been a great success.

We were on edge as the plane took off in some nasty inclement weather and just stared out the window as the aircraft continued to rise.

Higher and higher we climbed until piercing the thick layer of clouds and rising into what seemed like another world altogether. The sun was so bright that it lit up the entire plane and people squinted as they scrambled for the window shades.

I looked over at Curtis and said, without thinking, "It's always sunny above the clouds." In just a few moments I realized that I had uttered something profound. "Write that down," I told him.

The truth is, bad things happen to us all the time. As much as it is our own doing, we live in a world where we are surrounded by chaos. Experts say that 87% of everything we see, hear, and are exposed to is negative. Whether we're reading the paper, watching the news, sitting in the break room at work, or just overhearing a conversation at the local coffee shop, we are surrounded by whining and complaining. It takes a conscious effort not to be sucked in by it all.

Have you ever heard the term, "good-finder"? It's sort of self explanatory, but I'll help. It means look for "good" in others. It's in there somewhere. Every person has *something* good inside, wouldn't you say?

Working on becoming a good-finder means that you're constantly on the lookout to recognize and appreciate other people for the good things they do in life.

Ken Blanchard, in his book, *The One-Minute Manager* says, "Catch people doing something right! Then tell everyone about it."

Making the decision to become a Good-Finder puts you in the right frame of mind from the moment you wake up in the morning. If you've committed to an Appreciation Marketing Strategy that includes recognizing people all day long, then you're continuously "on the look out" for people and things to recognize and appreciate. This automatically makes you a better person. Try it.

Remember The Whiner from Chapter Four? The Whiner was always looking at the glass as half empty and always whining and complaining about something. Well, when you're a Good-Finder, you're really the opposite of The Whiner . . . you're The Winner.

One of the most positive people I have ever known is somebody whom I've never even met. Randy is always a pleasure to talk to. Again, though I've never actually met Randy in person, I've spoken to him on the phone so much that I consider him a dear friend. Through his amazing attitude, Randy always brightens my day and puts me in a great mood. And he does it without even trying. One of his greatest quotes comes when we say goodbye. He says, *"You have a great day, unless you have other plans!"*

I've been having regular conversations with Randy off and on now for about a year. I could write another entire book on positive, uplifting quotes out of that man's mouth. I've also received cards and uplifting emails from Randy, all of which I've saved. Randy is a huge business success, and I treasure the notes and messages he's sent me telling me that I'm on my way to the top. It's an amazing circumstance when you consider that this is a man I've never met, who has no vested interest in being nice to me. But it's even more amazing when you realize that all during our long-distance telephone friendship, Randy has been suffering from liver disease and was in need of a donor.

How could somebody going through all that be that positive? How could he be this giving and so selfless during a struggle for his own life? It's because he's someone who "gets it."

Jim Rohn, an internationally known success coach, author, and speaker says, "the same wind blows on us all. It's not what *happens* to us that determines our destiny. It's how we *handle* what happens to us. It's not the blowing of the wind. It's the set of the sail."

"I was raised by loving and wise parents who were children of the Depression," says Bob Wood, former Chairman and CEO of Chemtura Corporation. "We never had a lot, but I learned to be thankful for everything we did have. I learned that there is always someone who has less."

Wood's two most enduring lessons involved attitude and gratitude. "Any success that I have enjoyed in my life came as a direct result of those early lessons," he said. "The one thing in your life that you, and you alone, control, is your mind. My parents taught me that you can have anything in this life if you first believe it. What might seem like tragedy or failure in your life always gives you the ability to learn and become a better person. I'm thankful for that. Gratitude is an attitude, and attitude is everything."

My mother died of cancer at age 47. I was 27 at the time, and was angry at the world. I'd lie in bed at night and wonder aloud what it meant that "everything happens for a reason." Like, who made that up? What reason could there possibly be for my mother to be taken from my family at such a young age?

My mom was intelligent. In fact, she was one of the smartest people I ever knew. She didn't have an enemy in the world. This was evident at her wake when literally hundreds of people kept filing into the funeral home to pay their respects.

So my mom, a giver to the core, was erased from this earth prematurely and I'm supposed to believe "everything happens for a reason"?

I don't know if it was divine intervention or just the first intelligent choice I ever made in my life, but one night while laying there in bed, I made a decision. I figured I could question that unwritten law and live the rest of my life in anger and hatred, or I could seek out a "reason." I chose the latter.

I believe my mother died young because I was supposed to learn to live every day to its fullest. I'm supposed to wake up whistling. I'm supposed to be positive and full of life. And more importantly, I'm supposed to make other people understand that they can do it as well. That it's not a blessing. It's simply a choice.

That's a pretty empty glass that I was able to call partially full.

In the movie *Dumb and Dumber*, actor Jim Carrey's character asks a girl what the chances are that she'd ever be attracted to a guy like him. "One in a thousand?" he asks her. "More like one in a million," she answers. He looks shocked and then a huge smile comes to his face. "So you're telling me there's a chance!!" he exclaims with delight. Now *that's* a good-finder!

I've been carrying around a folded up piece of paper with a poem scribbled on it for several years. It was written by Terri McPherson (wisehearts.com) © 2000.

Choosing a Response

My ability to respond to a world,
over which I have no control,
is a powerful gift.
If I crumble in the face of adversity,
I have chosen to be
weak and beaten down.
If I soar to the heights of happiness,
I have chosen to fly.
Situations will choose me,
But they will never own me.
How I react to them will always
Be a matter of my own choice.

Do you look at a snowstorm as a bad thing or a chance to stay home and get some work done around the house? Do you complain that the roses have thorns, or can you appreciate that the thorns have roses? Do you grumble about your health, or are you happy to be alive? Do you gripe about having housework, or are you grateful you have a house? Today stretches ahead of you, waiting to be shaped and here you are the sculptor who gets to do the shaping.

It's always sunny above the clouds!

The Appreciator

. . . Sees Good Where Others Cannot

Is your glass half empty or half full? As practice, try to think of something really bad or negative in your life right now. Now what good can you find in that situation? Come on. Try hard. I promise you that there's something there. Maybe it's a lesson for you to learn, maybe it's just an inconvenience and isn't something bad at all. Once you master this ability, your life will be better. It's just a simple conditioning of the mind and it will set you apart from your competition in everything you do.

CHAPTER THIRTEEN

In My Next Life,
I'm Coming Back as ME!

"It's a sorry dog that won't wag its own tail."
— *Former U.S. Attorney General,*
Judge Griffin Bell

Ahh, what a thought! What a wonderful life you must be living to make a bold statement like that.

In this book we talked about Narcissus, who has a case of the "I love me" disease. We talked about The Topper, who always has to one-up you. And we concluded that there's no place for arrogance when it comes to real relationship building. My friend Kody Bateman would say, *"it's time to check your ego when you get to the door."*

But true success doesn't come unless you can appreciate yourself as well. There's nothing wrong with self appreciation; in fact, it's essential.

Whitney Houston sang, *"Learning to love yourself is the greatest love of all."*

You have to take care of yourself in life before you can hope to impact others. An easy example would be the last time you were about to take off in an airplane. The flight attendant, standing in the aisle, begins her routine of going over the safety information for the aircraft.

"If there's a sudden drop in cabin pressure, oxygen masks will drop from overhead. Using the elastic straps, secure the mask over your nose and mouth and breathe normally. Please be sure to secure your own mask before assisting others with theirs."

So what, exactly, does it mean to take care of yourself first?

When I was a little guy growing up, my mother always used to tell me, "If you think you're great, everyone else will too." I'll never forget those words, but I never knew what she meant. My mother was wise. She wasn't telling me to be an arrogant jerk. She was trying to get me to realize an inner confidence. She was trying to tell me that the opinion I had of myself would project itself to the world around me.

Like most people, I wasn't born with an overload of self confidence. In my neighborhood I wasn't the biggest, strongest, fastest, or smartest. All around me I saw and heard constant comparisons. And because I couldn't see myself ever living up to those comparisons, I became shy and withdrawn.

No matter how I tried to overcome those thoughts and feelings, there were still kids who could beat me up. There were still kids who got better grades in school. Had I been a little girl, there would have still been other girls who were prettier than me.

It's not until adulthood, or even parenthood, when you realize the impact society has on you if you just float down the river. Somewhere along the way, you have to make a decision to realize that you are a special and unique person. For me, it came with sports. By the time I was twelve I had developed a talent for hitting home runs. Nobody in the neighborhood could bang 'em out like me, and it was there where I was able to develop my confidence.

It continued through baseball, and ultimately men's league softball where I "thought I was the best" and I (almost always) was. That inner confidence projected itself and allowed me to turn my life around in a positive way by translating over into whatever else I did.

As I look back at my life, that home run confidence carried over to my ability to meet people and make friends. It carried over to my business. Suddenly, as more and more time passed, I began to be recognized.

Just the other night while reuniting with an old friend at a party he was hosting, he loudly announced to a group of bystanders that I had the Midas Touch! "Everything you touch turns to gold!" he said to my delight. Funny, I've been telling myself that for years! Finally somebody else agreed!

What is true greatness? It's the opinion you have of yourself. I can't place the quote, but at some time during the past ten years I heard some famous water-walking self-help guru say "the most important conversation you have is the conversation you have with yourself." Amen!

What do you see when you look in the mirror? To put a different spin on my mother's quote, "If you think you're a loser, everyone else will too." And since we only have 100% control over one thing in this world—what we think—what is your self talk telling you?

"I am nature's greatest miracle," wrote Og Mandino in *The Greatest Salesman in the World.* "I am not on this earth by chance. I am here for a purpose and that purpose is to grow into a mountain, not shrink to a grain of sand. Henceforth I will apply all my efforts to become the highest mountain of all and I will strain my potential until it cries for mercy."

Are you growing or shrinking? Your subconscious mind doesn't know the difference between what is real and what is imagined. Have you ever heard the old saying "you've lied so many times that now you're even starting to believe it"? It's true.

Richard Bliss Brooke, in his book *Mach II Starring You,* suggests that whatever "truths" you are experiencing in your life right now, you made it all up!

"What's true is that who you are and what you will accomplish with your life is a self-fulfilling prophecy. The truth is what you choose it to be and if you do not consciously choose, you subconsciously choose."

Brooke likens your life to a movie. You are the writer, you are the lead actor, you are the director and the producer. Your life is whatever you will it to be and if you don't make this realization and do something about it, then you just drift down the river of life and become part of somebody else's movie.

Recognize and appreciate yourself and the awesome power you possess to achieve whatever you wish. Heck, go for an Oscar!

The Appreciator

. . . Loves Life

I was in a bagel shop the other morning wearing a tee shirt that read: "In my next life, I'm coming back as ME!" The woman behind the counter read it, smiled, and said "wow, you must really like yourself a lot to wear a shirt that says that." "Yeah," I answered. "It's not a bad gig if you can get it!"

Get out a pen and a piece of paper and write down a list of five things that you just love about yourself! Don't worry, nobody's looking. It's not realistic to think you can appreciate others if you don't even appreciate yourself.

CHAPTER FOURTEEN

The Popcorn Principle

"If only you were making the right choices, doing those simple, little disciplines that would change your life for the better forever . . . where would you be five years from today?"

—Jeffrey Olson

By the age of five, most civilized human beings have experienced the guilty pleasure of eating popcorn. And you'd be hard pressed to find an adult who hasn't cooked up a batch.

One of my favorite things about making popcorn is that it stimulates all of the five senses in a way that nothing else can. You experience *hearing* in that unmistakable "pop . . . pop . . . pop." The unique *scent* of popcorn permeates any movie theater, tantalizing you to come to the snack line and have your credit card ready! *Taste*, of course, is also a sense that comes into play—although with popcorn your mouth generally begins to water even before you eat any. Finally, to add in the other two senses, you can *see* and *feel* popcorn and will never get it confused with anything else on earth.

More fascinating to me, though, is what we like to call "The Popcorn Principle," which holds true in popcorn, in business, and in life.

The Popcorn Principle simply states that certain actions repeated, when done in the proper sequence, will always yield the desired outcome.

Growing up in the 1970's, I first experienced popcorn in my mother's kitchen the "old fashioned way." With no instant popcorn, no microwave ovens, or heat poppers, I used to watch mom heat up oil in a pan on the stove. She'd then pour in the kernels, hold the lid on, and slide the pan back and forth over the flame until the popping began. Once the corn started pushing the lid off the pan, she'd pour the whole batch into a bowl and pour on the salt and melted butter! Oh baby! Here go those senses again!

My co-author's generation did it much differently when it ushered in the new age of popcorn. Today we take a flat paper package from the box, remove the plastic wrapping, place it on the carousel inside the microwave— "this end up" —and press the button that says "popcorn." The salt, butter, cheese, caramel, spice, or any other specified popcorn flavor is all predetermined inside that little paper bag full of seeds. Just put it in, press the buttons, and step back.

The Popcorn Principle states that if you follow these directions to a tee, you'll end up with a perfect bowl of popcorn every time. Why, then, do people still mess it up?

The challenge with this principle, you see, is that people don't like to follow directions.

What would happen if you put the popcorn into the microwave, followed all the directions perfectly, but got impatient and took the bag out before it started popping? "It's not working!" you're thinking as you stand there and stare through the glass door.

What would happen if you wanted it extra hot, so you decided to let it cook longer than the allotted time? This conjures up images of a fiery black, charred bag being rushed out onto the back porch. Have you ever tried to get the smell of burnt popcorn out of your kitchen?

Then we have the group who wants things fast, fast, fast! Who has time to wait two minutes for the popcorn? We're going to try a blow torch to expedite the process!

These examples seem silly because we all know how simple it is to make a bag of microwave popcorn. If he follows the directions on the box, every rational human being has "faith" that the ends will justify the means. This is actually the use of the Sixth Sense, which is faith, belief, or intuition.

It's important to understand that The Popcorn Principle also holds true in your business and personal life.

In his best-selling book, *The Slight Edge*, Jeffrey Olson talks about the consequences, both positive and negative, of small disciplines repeated.

To put this in perspective, if you went out to a fast food joint for lunch and hammered down two burgers, large fries, and a large soda, chances are you wouldn't drop dead of a heart attack on the car ride home. But with this small act repeated—say a few times a day for a few years—chances are good that you might.

You are unlikely to contract lung cancer if you go outside right now and smoke a cigarette. But if you chain smoke a few packs a day for a few years, you'll greatly improve those odds.

Everyone has experienced watching his credit card balance get higher and higher each month without even making a purchase. It's called compounding interest (aka paying $362 for a roll of breath mints you ate a year ago!) And it's just another example of The Popcorn Principle.

Let's change the tone to a positive one.

If you join the gym on January 1, and show up for a full workout, will you go home with the body you desire? NO! You'll go home with a whole lot of sore muscles and a little voice that says, "Are you crazy? Don't go back there!!" It's those who find a way to ignore or suppress that little voice, who go back to the gym every day—even if just for a few minutes a day—and develop an exercise habit, who eventually—over time—achieve the body and fitness level they desire.

A financial planner will advise you to invest your money in such a way that it will continue to grow. Isn't that a foreign concept? You mean if I invested one thousand dollars six years ago, I'd have six thousand dollars today? Yep.

So how does all this relate to Appreciation Marketing?

Simple. If you begin to utilize an AMS that includes saying thank you, being a more likable person, being a giver, sending random notes and greeting cards for no particular reason, expressing genuine gratitude through heartfelt phone calls and unexpected small gifts, acknowledging and appreciating yourself and all the things in your life, then you—just like you did with that bag of popcorn—will reap the benefits of an abundant life. This will carry forth in both your business and your personal life, guaranteed.

Will it happen in five minutes? The exciting news is that it might! But don't get discouraged if it doesn't. The speed at which your popcorn pops, so to speak, will depend heavily on how well you've practiced the Appreciation Marketing principles before you read this book.

Will it happen over time? Absolutely, one hundred percent guaranteed.

The secret is simple: choose and practice a few simple disciplines—negative or positive—compound them daily, and then project your life forward.

Whether you'd like to improve your health, your relationship with your family, your faith, your friends, your finances, or your business, the answer lies within The Popcorn Principle.

And don't focus your time or energy on the few kernels at the bottom of the bag that didn't pop. Instead, enjoy the corn!

Begin to apply random acts of appreciation—STARTING TODAY.

The Appreciator

... Practices Proper Habits

What random acts of appreciation can you apply starting today? Go ahead and make a list of just three.
Then DO THEM!

CHAPTER FIFTEEN

Build it, and They Will Come

(Formulate *Your* AMS)

"Doubt will take you out of action;
Action will take you out of doubt."

—*Pat Hintze*

W ho doesn't remember that prophetic whisper, emanating from the corn fields in Dyersville, Iowa?

"Build it, and they will come."

The overriding theme of the 1989 "Best Picture of the Year" nominee, *Field of Dreams*, was to never give up on your dreams, no matter how much effort it takes

In terms of this book, the *'it'* refers to your Appreciation Marketing Strategy. The *'they,'* of course, represents people; people with an infinite supply of positive energy that will result in an abundance of goodwill in both your personal and professional life.

Zig Ziglar says, "You have to *be*, before you can *do*. And you have to *do*, before you can *have*." We all understand the *have* part. We all know what we want to *have* in life.

But as Zig suggests, we can't get to the *have* part without the other two first.

So whatever it is that you desire to be and eventually have, it can all start with your AMS as the vehicle; as the "do." And in order to "do" an AMS, you have to "be" a grateful and appreciative person. I think we've thoroughly addressed that issue.

So here's where the rubber meets the road. When challenges arise, you can do one of three things. You can *worry*. You can *hope*. Or you can *create*. You create by taking action and we suggest that you begin your action by creating your own personal AMS.

It goes back to the previous chapter on The Popcorn Principle. If it's all about the small actions repeated, what should those small actions be? Let's do that now.

Implementing Your Appreciation Marketing Strategy (AMS)

STEP ONE: *WHAT?*

Start out your own personal AMS by first determining *what* it is that you actually wish to accomplish both personally and professionally. This list is ever-growing and isn't something that you can just lackadaisically jot down off the top of your head.

Get out a journal, or a notebook, and spend some time with this step. Carefully create some short term, long term, and "heart's desire" goals, write them down, and attach deadlines.

Remember, "a goal without a deadline is a wish."

STEP TWO: *WHY?*

Once you have created your list of desires, take some more time and ask yourself *why* you want each of these outcomes. Again, don't let your negative self-talk tell you that this is a futile exercise. Achieving all your goals won't come easily, and your "why" is what will help you through the challenges that arise. It's this step that so many people fail to take.

One of my favorite quotes is from Gary Ryan Blair. He says, "The person who knows *how* will always have a job. And they'll always be working for the person who knows *why*."

STEP THREE: *WHEN?*

When, exactly, do you plan to get started on this journey? Implementing your AMS isn't a daunting task. And considering you can begin instantly the second you make contact with another human being, why not just get it rolling right now?

Want to create an explosion? Use TNT *(Today, Not Tomorrow)*.

STEP FOUR: *WHO?*

Who are the people in your life, who are ready and waiting to be appreciated? Create a contact management system for yourself and fill it with every human being you know—or ever have known. Classify these people, of course, into groups such as friends, family, colleagues, customers, associates, etc. But be sure not to leave a single stone unturned. You'll be adding to this list as your memory is jogged, but you'll also make it a goal to add to it daily through the new people you come into contact with.

There are many places where you can create such a contact management system. We use an excellent one that is provided with our service through SendOutCards.com.

STEP FIVE: *HOW?*

If you've read this far, then the *How* is probably oozing out of your eyeball sockets by now.

Start in small increments. Don't jump into your contact manager and try to recognize and appreciate everybody with one fell swoop! It doesn't work that way.

Instead make a plan based on how many minutes each day you are willing to commit to your new AMS.

For starters, be conscious of birthdays and commit to somehow recognize people on that day. No, we don't get as excited about our birthdays as we get older, but we always appreciate when somebody acknowledges that special day. And, more importantly, we always remember who does.

Who just popped into your head? See? We all have at least one or two people who always remember us on our birthdays. They either send cards or call us on the phone. Doesn't it make you feel good to stir up that memory?

I fondly remember that my father's Aunt Millie would send me a birthday card every single year with a check in it, until she passed away when I was 35. I still have some of those cards in a drawer. My Aunt Janice and my wife's grandfather, Ray Byrd, were then left as the only birthday cards I could count on receiving every year in the mailbox. (Selected family members do still *hand* me a card).

If a card is out of the question for your AMS, then a phone call is second best. I can count on five or six phone calls from family members every year, but the only person not related to me who recognizes me is a man named Tom DeFelice.

I met Tom at a business conference in Dallas, Texas in 1998. During our brief conversation he asked me what my birthday was, and I told him August 30. I thought it was a strange question at the time, but since that day, and though we never really became close friends, he has called me on it every year since—usually leaving a voice message. It's no wonder that Tom DeFelice has become a legend as a big-time real estate success in the Warwick, Rhode Island area.

So become a collector of birthdays, and recognize people on them. You don't have to get elaborate. Just do something! I'd like to point out that since formulating my own AMS just two years ago, I received nearly 200 birthday cards in the mail on my 44th last summer. Hmm, what you give out really is what you get back.

Sending thank you notes is also a huge part of an effective AMS. The "expected" thank yous are crucial, but it's the "unexpected" thank yous that set you apart. What's an *unexpected* thank you? Think about it. If you go out of your way for somebody, or give somebody a gift, you *expect* a thank you. When it comes, it's appreciated but, again, it was *expected*.

An unexpected thank you is exactly that. You didn't expect to get it. Few people understand the power of the unexpected thank you because so few people have ever received one. Your job is to send them.

Who do you know who has had an impact on your life? Maybe it's a former teacher or coach. Maybe it's a parent, a grandparent, or a sibling. Maybe it's an old neighbor, a pastor, or an old friend. How about contacting these people to say thank you? It's difficult to do this by telephone, so a handwritten letter or greeting card would fit best here.

My youngest brother Jason recently sent me a fifteen page letter telling me how much of a positive impact I've made on his life. From being a big brother, to his Little League Baseball coach, he went on and on recalling past events and situations where I said or did something that helped shape his life for the better. To say I was blown away would be an understatement. I was bawling my eyes out. This letter, this act of appreciation, is one of the most special and unexpected gifts I've ever received in my lifetime.

Since receiving that letter from my brother, I've been prompted to send those unexpected thank yous to people who have been instrumental in my growth. It's an awesome power to realize that I have the ability to make other people feel as good as I felt when I read Jason's note.

Other unexpected thank yous can be sent to someone who provided you with a great product or service. How about somebody who helped you out with something recently? Maybe it was somebody who greeted you with a smile. Maybe there's somebody at the office who, in just doing their job, goes unnoticed and un-thanked. If you put your mind to it, you can find cause to thank somebody for something every day. Your life gets better immediately because of the feelings you receive on the "giving" end. You'll feel fulfilled just knowing that your simple gesture could be brightening someone else's day.

Make this a habit and watch what happens in your business and personal life.

Last Mother's Day I took my wife and two daughters to a special new restaurant in our area for brunch. It was the single worst dining experience of my life and in the end I paid over $200 for "the brunch that never was." Later that night I began writing a letter to the general manager, voicing my displeasure and wishing him luck staying in business. Then I came to my senses. What the heck was I doing? What would I hope to accomplish with a letter like that? Clearly that's the *opposite* of appreciation.

So I tore up the letter and instead wrote out a greeting card to my favorite restaurant. Inside the card I wrote:

> *To Jimmy and all my friends at Sake,*
>
> *Most people spend all their time complaining, and I'm sure you all get your fair share. I just wanted to let you know that it's people like all of you that have helped make Sake my favorite restaurant on the planet (and I've been to a lot)!!*
>
> *Thanks for always making me feel as though I'm among friends. The food's not too bad either!!*
>
> *I'm proud to be your #1 customer!*
> *Tommy*

Just writing out the card made me feel 100% better. Then, a week later, I walked into the restaurant to pick up a take-out order. I had forgotten about the card.

The staff started whispering to one another and the general manager, Jimmy, came toward me at a brisk pace. With a big smile on his face, he grabbed my hand and embraced me with a hug.

"Thank you," he said. As I suddenly remembered the card, staff members started appearing out of nowhere thanking me for what was (to me) a simple gesture. To them, though, it was ten times more meaningful. I was then introduced to the restaurant's owner for the first time. He had my card in his hand, and paid for my dinner that night. Every time I've walked into that restaurant since, I've been treated like royalty. It wasn't my intention. My intention was to send an *unexpected* thank you to some people who, in my mind, deserved it.

It's my opinion that the unexpected thank you produces more feelings of appreciation and gratitude than any other form.

Your AMS should also include the simplest forms of appreciation that don't take any time at all. Smile, for starters. It blows my mind when I stand in line at a coffee shop and wait my turn. Manners seem to be at an all time low and smiles seem to be scarce. Appreciation includes people who take your order. They deserve a smile, a friendly voice, and a please and thank you as much as anybody else. Think about that and begin to implement that plan immediately.

I'm a fan of the two-handed handshake and hugs when appropriate. Look into peoples' eyes when you speak to them. Really listen when they talk and don't glance around the room. Yes, these are forms of appreciation. Think about the last time you had a conversation with someone who didn't extend you the courtesy of being polite or paying attention to what you had to say.

Here's something that you've probably never done, but the superstars of Appreciation Marketing do all the time. When you hire somebody and they do excellent work for you, in addition to thanking them properly, take a few minutes and type up a professional-looking testimonial on your personal (or your company) letterhead. Then sign it. This simple act will come back to you tenfold.

We discussed, way back in Chapter Two, the effectiveness of gift giving. You don't want to bankrupt yourself buying gifts for people every day of the week. But start your AMS by committing to send out just one small gift per week. Start with something under ten dollars. Give it in person, or leave it for someone with a card or a note. Get creative here and really set yourself apart. Small gifts could include brownies, doughnuts and bagels, cups of coffee, gift cards, candies, books, magazines, flowers, and things of this nature. Be sure to give these small gifts as an act of appreciation. Do it because it's the right thing to do. Do it and *expect* nothing back.

It's crucial to your AMS that you do not include business cards, logos, or promotional materials of any kind with these gifts! Remember the phony dog poop cake in Chapter Five!

As we begin our new lives of appreciation, it's vitally important not to neglect those closest to home. Sometimes, in our effort to recognize the positive things around us, we take the most important ones for granted. We're talking about our spouses, our children, our parents, and our siblings. Many times we make the assumption that those people know how much we care about them, so we don't make the effort to communicate it. I work hard to fight that battle every day. These are the people who might just deserve your appreciation the most, and they crave it as well. Remember, appreciation begins at home.

The biggest regret that people carry around, generally, is that they neglected to appreciate someone and then that someone dies. The greatest thing you can do for another person, and for yourself, is to express your gratitude and your feelings to the people in your life—while they are still in your life!

There's no room for ego or selfishness where your AMS is concerned either. What does this mean? Is there some negative influence in your life? Are there people around you that you just do not like? Why not just appreciate them anyway? One of The 7 Habits of Highly Effective People is *Seek first to understand, then to be understood.* Surely, you can find some little quality to appreciate in even the worst of people. This is the most challenging part of your journey, but one that can be life changing. It was Gandhi who said, *"Always aim at complete harmony of thought and word and deed. Always aim at purifying your thoughts and everything will be well."*

Finally, just use your imagination. Apply an attitude of gratitude to everything that you do and don't forget to appreciate yourself along the way.

Our wish for everybody is that you can wake up singing, spread happiness wherever you go, and live a long life full of positive blessings. What would that feel like? Live a life of appreciation and attract those same grateful feelings from everyone around you. What you give out is what you get back in this life and we all have 100% control over that.

For having made that discovery, we are eternally grateful.

Epilogue

"It's not what you are that holds you back, it's what you think you're not."

—*Denis Waitley*

Dr Steven Covey says that one of the best ways to learn a principle is to teach it.

It is on that million dollar advice that Curtis and I ask that you pass this knowledge along to your staff, your associates, your friends, your families and everyone you come in contact with.

The best way, of course, to teach these principles is to practice them regularly. If you formulate and commit to following your own personal Appreciation Marketing Strategy, you will naturally become an example to others through your own actions.

If you smile at someone, someone smiles back.

If you do a good deed, someone will do one in return.

If you remember birthdays, people will remember yours.

If you care, others will care as well.

It's all in your hands now. Remember, the opposite laws apply to these principles as well. What you give out is what you get back. (Have we said this often enough yet?)

Now *you* say it. Write it down. Say it again. Jot that down on the back of your business card and post it somewhere where you can look at it every single day.

If you've been relatively appreciative already, then you can hit the ground running. But it doesn't matter how far gone you might be, it's never too late to appreciate. So shake off the cobwebs and start a new existence.

We made a big claim when we entitled this book *"How to Achieve Greatness Through Gratitude."* We've been asked: What is greatness? Greatness can have a different meaning to different people. The *American Heritage Dictionary* has multiple definitions itself. So we'll just ask you to take your pick of the following: remarkable, outstanding, significant, important, superior in quality or character, noble, powerful, influential, eminent, distinguished, grand, enthusiastic, skillful, or first-rate.

Now that you've grabbed hold of the meaning that makes the most sense to you, go ahead and decide where you'd like to actually achieve it.

Whether you desire to be a great business owner, a great salesperson, a great employee, a great marketer, a great conversationalist, a great friend, a great spouse, a great lover, a great parent, a great role model, a great business partner, a great leader, a great follower, or just a great person in general . . . you now hold the key.

To achieve that greatness, start with gratitude and appreciation. And you may as well start now. In the words of the great Mark Twain, "Twenty years from now you will be more disappointed by the things that you didn't do than by the ones you did do. So throw off the bowlines.

Sail away from the safe harbor. Catch the trade winds in your sails. Explore. Dream. Discover."

We appreciate you.

But you knew that!

About the Authors

TOMMY WYATT was born in upstate New York the oldest of three boys. After a few family moves—his father worked for IBM (I've Been Moved)—he established roots in Newtown, CT where he graduated high school (somehow).

From the ages of 18-22, which included six years of college, Tommy had twenty different jobs (watch for *"Unemployable"* coming soon at a bookstore near you). At 23, he took an hourly-wage job as a sports writer at a small weekly newspaper called *The Newtown Bee.* During a ten-year career at *The Bee*, he followed a passion for people and for sports, coached Little League Baseball and starred in men's league softball. Midway through his journalism career, Tommy became sports editor and his work received honors from The New England Press Association in each of the five years he ran the sports section.

In 1998, Tommy was introduced to network marketing and subsequently walked away from a job he loved. It would be his last. Through network marketing and direct sales, he grew an organization of tens of thousands of distributors that spanned seven countries. During that time, he traveled the world speaking in front of large audiences and training on the principles of relationships, networking, and team building.

Throughout his tenure in the industry, which saw him reach the top 1% globally, Tommy lectured at many prestigious universities including Harvard, Yale, and the University of Connecticut on the topic of entrepreneurship.

Before co-authoring this book, he wrote (but never published) *"We Were All Sports Heroes,"* and contributed a chapter in Jack Canfield & Mark Victor Hansen's *"Chicken Soup for the Network Marketer's Soul"* as well as being featured in many other industry publications.

Tommy is currently a corporate trainer and top producer for SendOutCards. His love and genuine passion for what he does come through clearly in his seminars as well as his daily routine.

He lives in Connecticut with his wife, Michele, and their daughters Sydney and Cassidy.

CURTIS LEWSEY grew up in upstate New York as well, with an older brother and two younger sisters.

At the age of 15, Curtis was asked to play for an elite summer baseball league that traveled North America. There where he realized that hard work and persistence were essential to take his game to the next level.

Coming from a small town with only 85 students in his high school senior class, Curtis was recruited to play Division I college baseball for Sacred Heart University. His work ethic helped him work his way from the junior varsity squad his freshman year to varsity team captain by his senior year.

In his junior year at SHU, Curtis was informed that he'd have to find a way to pay for his own tuition. So he started his own business on campus and earned enough income around his hectic schedule to pay for his final two years.

A week after graduating SHU in 2005, Curtis lost his brother Silas to a freak dirt bike accident. This tragic event made him realize that life can be cut short at anytime.

He took a sales position with Cintas Corporation out of college and immediately earned awards as the top sales-man in the company. Despite that success, Curtis never felt right working for someone else. He quit the job and started a distributorship with SendOutCards in April 2007. He is now a corporate trainer there, and has a passion for helping others attract greatness by teaching the appreciation principles of this book.

He lives in Connecticut with his wife, Heather.

Acknowledgments

"If you see a turtle on a fencepost, you know he had some help along the way."

—*Unknown*

In a book about appreciation, this turns out to be the most important and appropriate chapter of all. Both Curtis and I have a laundry list of people who have had a major hand in our journey.

Our equal thanks go to:

Kody Bateman, founder and CEO of SendOutCards, for understanding the importance of the appreciation philosophy and founding a company and a mechanism that has changed both our lives forever. And for giving us a platform to be able to internalize this concept as well.

Jordan Adler, author of *Beach Money*, for introducing us to that company and for your help in the book "process." Don't know where we'd be without you buddy.

Anthony Robbins, whose "Unleash the Power Within" seminar in April 2007 gave us both the spark to realize that we needed to make a career change.

Roger Barnett, CEO of Shaklee Corp, who gave us those tickets, and who gave us a brief look into a world we never knew existed.

Jim Jacobus, who said "you should write a book and call it *'You Should Have Said Thank You.'*" We were listening, Jim.

Sandy Shepard, for all your help with our semicolon addiction! What you give out really is what you get back. We appreciate you.

To our photographer Mike Loring, our typesetter Marian Hartsough, our website designer Marie DeSalvo, our graphic designer Solomon Dauber, our trademark attorney Jamie Shelden, Peter Bowerman for writing *The Well-Fed Self Publisher*, and Shelly Sapyta at BookMasters. We couldn't have done it without you!

All of our BNI friends and colleagues who are a continuous source of inspiration and support.

To literally thousands of SendOutCards friends and business partners who help us spread this message every single day. You know who you are! Thank you for your vision of the future!

And to all the Appreciators in the world. You make it a better place!

Tommy's Acknowledgments

My wife Michele, whose patience, support, and understanding—even when I know it hasn't been easy—has been the backbone of what is becoming a major success story. I know I don't thank you enough and I'll do better. When I proclaim myself to be "the happiest man in the world," it wouldn't be so without you. I love you.

Sydney and Cassidy, my two angels, who are growing up way too fast, but hopefully learning these important principles along the way. I'll never stop reaching—and it's all for you.

Donna Lee Wyatt, my mom, whose inspiration could fill another 100 pages in this book. Though I never believed her, she told me that I was special every day of my life. Some of her unfulfilled dreams, which I am living for her, included writing a book and traveling the world. Her leaving this earth prematurely allowed me to understand the true meaning of life. I love you mom.

Tommy Wyatt Sr., my dad, and my biggest cheerleader on the sidelines. He spent his life giving me good advice, none of which did I follow. I know you're proud dad, and nothing makes me happier. Sorry for being an impossible son.

My brothers Jeff and Jason and the rest of my family, on both sides, who have always been supportive of everything I've done. I'm blessed.

Fred Stevens, who took a petrified 33-year-old MLM rookie, stuck him in front of the room, and gave him the confidence to excel in business and in life and the passion to reach for the stars.

Chuck Tilson, who harassed me every day for a month to look at a network marketing presentation in 1998, thus rescuing me from an otherwise ordinary life.

Cindy Miller who, after the first time I spoke in front of a room, told me that I was destined for greatness. I never forgot that.

Jim Steiwing, who gave me a personal hand-written letter after my very first "big" training seminar. Your words of encouragement inspired me more than you'll ever know. I still have the letter.

Len Becchetti, my Little League coach in 1974. Kids don't get to pick their coach. I just got lucky that summer. Thank you for the Rookie of the Year trophy (I still have it) and for having a positive impact on my life. I'm paying it forward.

Bill Brassard, who hired me for my first (and last) "real job" as a sportswriter and helped me develop a love for story telling.

Scudder Smith, who first exposed me to "the good life."

People like Kody Bateman, Erik Laver, Jordan Adler, Randy Davis, Roger Barnett, Pat Hintze, Angel Torres, Steve Schulz, Joe Mitchell, Russ and Vince Widger (and the big man), and Shawn Gray who have inspired me through your actions.

Some 20,000 people who have believed in me enough to follow over the past eleven years, and mostly my SOC team leaders of today. You all may think that I inspire you, but it's clearly the other way around.

Curtis Lewsey, my business partner. You might be 18 years younger than me, brother, but you are a huge inspiration in my life. Your drive, determination, and energy keep me motivated to do more. I couldn't have picked a better partner. Let's change the world!

Heather McKillop Lewsey: I know how hard it is to be apart from your spouse for days and nights on end. The reason most people fail in life is because of the lack of support from their "significant other." Curtis will never fail in life. Thank you for that.

And finally, Boomer, my little buddy. You exemplified appreciation and gratitude more than anyone I've met in my entire lifetime. No matter my mood, you always greeted me with love and changed my state. Though you've been gone for years now, I cry happy tears every time I think of your smiling eyes and your wagging tail. The whole world can learn from man's best friend. You were mine.

Curtis'
Acknowledgments

Heather for my strength, my everything, my "why" in life! Thank you for always being there for me with support, understanding and love. You mean the world to me and I'm looking forward to sharing an incredible life together. You raise me up and allow me to live with passion. I love you.

Mom and Dad, for all your love and encouragement. I can't thank you enough for never doubting my dreams or holding me back. I appreciate and love you both so much!

Mr. Beck, for recognizing me as a leader and telling me so. You expected nothing but my best, taught me responsibility and a life lesson I will never forget: "Don't let your lows get you too low or your highs too high."

Coach Medici, for the Greg Koubek basketball camp scholarship in the summer of 1995. That could not have come at a more crucial time in my life. I will never forget what that week did for my confidence. Thank You.

Mr. Godlewski, for scouting our game, Greenwich vs. Stillwater, in the spring of 1998. You being there set in motion a string of events that led me to the opportunity to travel the county and play the game I love, landing in Connecticut at Sacred Heart University, and meeting my future soul mate.

Jon Cohen for creating an internship and hiring me out of college. Thank you for helping me focus on my purpose and always pushing me beyond what I thought was possible.

Rob Duell, for always having the answers, in a light-hearted, grand scheming kind of way. My stress level seemed to disappear within seconds of a conversation. "Curtis, all you have to do is Grand Scheme it."

Johnny Morton, for your continuing support and advice. Uplifted, motivated and inspired are a few words to describe what kind of state I am in after talking with you. Thank you being a great brother.

Tommy Wyatt, for being you. In the Sacred Heart baseball program players were asked a series of questions. One was "If you could have lunch with anyone, who would it be?" My answer was "Tommy Wyatt." You had a lifestyle that I dreamed about and a personality that I wanted to emulate. It's crazy how things unfold. I'm honored to call you my business partner and friend. Thank You!

Tom & Holly McKillop, for being so welcoming. It's a pleasure to call you family. So many amazing memories to come.

Andrea, Deana and Valerie for your support and love. I am so proud to call you my sisters.

I would also like to thank Kap and G, Uncle Rob and Aunt Mary, Grandma Mann, Grandpa and Alice, Grandma and Papa, Nana, and all of my SOC team leaders who have become much more than just business partners. You're my friends.

A Final Note From Curtis

On the night of May 20, 2005 I was in Lakewood, NJ to play in our conference baseball tournament when my dad and my sister Deana walked into the hotel and told me that my big brother Silas was involved in a freak dirt bike accident that took his life. He was only 23.

I was crushed. With any tragic death, especially when it's someone so close to you, it brings out the big question of "why?" It's difficult to cope with the theory that "everything happens for a reason" after an incident of that magnitude.

I'll never forget being at the funeral when my father said to me, "Silas lived more life in his 23 years than most do in a normal lifetime." That comment made me realize that we all should wake up every day with passion and live it like it might be our last. It occurred to me that people lose friends and family members every day. I can't imagine a worse tragedy than losing a loved one without having had the chance to say 'I love you and appreciate you.'

Tommy and I are now blessed to be able to help inspire others to implement more appreciation into their personal and professional lives in order to strengthen relationships. This is extremely rewarding and drives us to help let millions of people around the world in on what the superstars of their industries already know.

I hope we've struck a nerve.

Recommended Reading

In our travels we are continually asked for a list of recommended reading. We're happy to provide a list of books that have been instrumental to our journey. We've even referred to many of them in this book.

In no particular order (read 'em all):

The Slight Edge, Jeffrey Olson

The 29% Solution, Dr. Ivan Misner

The Greatest Salesman in the World, Og Mandino

Unlimited Referrals, Bill Cates

Business by Referral, Dr. Ivan Misner

Hug Your Customers, Jack Mitchell

Beach Money, Jordan Adler

The Secret, Rhonda Byrne

The Science of Getting Rich, Wallace Wattles

The Likeability Factor, Tim Sanders

Breaking Barriers, Leif Becker

Mach II With Your Hair on Fire, Richard Bliss Brooke

Dig Your Well Before You're Thirsty, Harvey Mackay

The Unbreakable Human Spirit, Randy Gonzales Jr.

Unlimited Power, Anthony Robbins

The Greatest Networker in the World, John Milton Fogg

Think and Grow Rich, Napoleon Hill

How to Win Friends and Influence People, Dale Carnegie

The 7 Habits of Highly Effective People, Dr. Steven Covey

The Go-Giver, Bob Burg & John David Mann

Everyday Greatness, Dr. Steven Covey

The Five Major Pieces to the Life Puzzle, Jim Rohn

The Seven Spiritual Laws of Success, Deepak Chopra